The Data-Driven Union

Transforming you credit union with a
data-driven decision culture

By Michael Cochrum

CMRG Publishing

McKinney, TX

Illustrations: Michael Cochrum

Cover Design: Michael Cochrum

Cover Art: istockphoto

Table of Contents

What is a data-driven decision culture? 5

My Personal Data Journey 24

The Case for Data-Driven Decision Transformation 43

The Big Data Hype 65

Common Transformation Roadblocks and Hurdles............................85

Creating an Enterprise Data-Driven Culture Transformation

Strategy...101

Data Integration and Modeling: Part I, Definition of

Important Terms...125

Data Integration and Modeling: Part II, Important

Considerations..143

Analytics: Descriptive, Predictive and Prescriptive............................166

Data Visualization 186

Appendix I...208

Acknowledgements 209

About the Author...212

Chapter 1

What is a data-driven decision culture?

Decades ago, my grandpa, Paul Price made a business decision. After returning from WWII, a purple-heart recipient, he resumed work on his small farm outside Mayfield, Ky. Grandpa was a strong and muscular man who exemplified to me what work ethic and dedication looked like in mid-twentieth century America. But, for some reason, farming was not where he wanted to end up in life. He wanted something more for his family, so he and his brother Bill moved to town and started a plumbing company, Price's Plumbing. As it turns out, that plumbing company provided he and his brother a level of prosperity, well into the late 1980's, until they eventually both retired. Sadly, most of their sons and daughters went on to do other things with their lives and the company no longer exists today.

I had many discussions with my grandpa over the years when he would allow me to ride along in his truck as he made service calls for people in town. I suppose we had a discussion at some point about why he decided to start a plumbing business, but I can't remember it if we did. I don't remember him mentioning creating a business plan, conducting a market analysis, or running financial projections. He just worked. And every time I went to visit him, he was working, so I worked too. The phone would ring, he'd jump in his truck and go to work, sometimes even on holidays like Thanksgiving and Christmas. He made a good living and he and his brother earned an excellent reputation among their customers. I learned a lot from my grandpa about work ethic and integrity.

To be sure, Price's Plumbing Company did not have a data-driven decision culture. My Grandpa wasn't a Data Scientist and would probably be a little disappointed to find out that is what I had become, if he were still alive today. It wouldn't make much sense to him. That's because my grandpa dropped out of school in the sixth grade and I came to find out when I was older that he didn't even read well, if at all. That doesn't change the fact that he was a successful and well thought of business man, but you wouldn't know that today because his company no longer exists. While businesses can exist without data-driven decisions, companies can't survive and grow in a competitive environment without using data to inform and support business decisions.

If you head south of Mayfield and drive about 150 miles you will arrive at the headquarters of another plumbing company, Rescue Rooter, in Memphis, TN. Rescue Rooter, a nationwide brand, was founded in 1975 as a family-owned business in California[1]. This company was started just ten years before my grandpa's company went out of business. The difference is that someone in this business saw the opportunity, on a national level, for on-time, quality plumbing service; the exact same services that Price's Plumbing offered just two and a half hours to the north. What causes two companies, that basically start the same way, to end up so differently in the end? It can't simply be that one worked harder than the other because I can't imagine someone working harder than my Grandpa. No offense to all my plumbing friends out there, but it's not brain surgery, so it can't be education level. It's not just vision and leadership, because my grandpa was a strong leader in many ways. Finally, plumbing technology hasn't really changed significantly since the elevated toilet water tank was introduced in 1910[2], so it can't be solely innovation. We must agree that the difference here is the ability to visualize information beyond the cranking of a wrench, or the fundamental skills required to make a business successful.

To successfully grow a small, family-owned business into a national brand requires more than hard work, more than great service, and more than satisfied customers; it requires business decisions made using relevant data. Credit union's obviously do not provide the same services

---

[1] https://www.ars.com/about-us/history

[2] https://www.johncflood.com/blog/general/history-of-plumbing-timeline

as plumbing companies, but the decision-making process is not that much different between a credit union leader and any other entrepreneur. In fact, most credit unions began their journey in the same way a family business is started, a handful of individuals with a common bond who joined together to provide a service for the people in their community. This is just as true for the $10 million credit union as it is for the multi-billion-dollar credit union. The primary difference between the large and small financial institutions is how its leadership makes decisions about how to serve the market.

In a 2011 study of 3,000 organizations in 100 countries across 30 industries, MIT Sloan Management Review and the IBM Institute for Business Value researchers found that top performing organizations "use [data] analytics five times more than lower performers."[3] The study further found that top performing organizations are two times more likely to use data analytics to guide future strategies as well as guide day-to-day operations. In other words, data analytics is embedded in their business, is part of the organization's vernacular and is an expected component in decision making. My observation has been, over the past seven or eight years, that credit unions are struggling to adopt data analytics strategies for several reasons. The good news is that there is an amazing opportunity to change the competitive landscape for credit unions as more credit union leaders adopt data-driven decision cultures and work toward transformation. The time for change is now.

---

[3] https://sloanreview.mit.edu/article/big-data-analytics-and-the-path-from-insights-to-value/

****

So far, we have illustrated the difference between the 'have's' and the 'have not's' when it comes to data-driven decision making, but we haven't really defined what a data-driven decision culture looks like in the real world. A data-driven decision culture is one where decision-makers act on a combination of data and intuition rather than solely on the decision-maker's experience and expertise. That definition seems a bit ambiguous and requires a little 'fleshing out' with, perhaps, some reality-based examples. Consider the following hypothetical illustration.

Don Kirkpatrick has been President/CEO of Hiawatha Hills Credit Union for the last ten years. The credit union has $470 million in assets and has seen 5%, year over year, asset growth for the past 5 years straight. Mr. Kirkpatrick has gathered his leadership team to discuss performance goals for the next year. Sidney Lane is the credit union's V.P. of Marketing and she has been with the credit union for four years. She came to HHCU from a smaller credit union in town where she was Member Service and Engagement Manager. Roger Baker is the credit unions CFO/COO. Roger was the Chief Lending Officer for the credit union before Don was promoted from the CFO/COO position to CEO, when he was then promoted to fill Don's spot. Finally, Beth Rogers is the Chief Lending Officer who joined the leadership team last year, having recently been the V.P. of Lending for a local community bank. Beth is the sixth CLO the credit union has had since Roger's promotion.

Kirkpatrick begins the meeting, "Well team, it's that time of year again. We need to set goals for the next year. I really don't care how we get there as long as we hit the $500 million asset threshold. I've been chasing that down since I became CEO, ten years ago. Plus, asset growth provides us the scale we need to trigger rapid growth and provide a higher level of service to our members."

Ms. Lane responded, "I think we can do that if we invest more into marketing. We need to increase our brand awareness. I'm going to need to increase our marketing budget by $120,000 in order to run a year-long campaign that I believe will draw in more members and deposits."

"How many members?", asked Roger, "We're going to need a lot. It seems we are losing more members today than we're gaining, thanks to those Indirect borrowers who don't stick around very long."

"Now wait a minute, Roger", Beth responds, "How could I possibly achieve the loan growth goals I've been given without Indirect Lending. It's not like people are walking in off the street and applying for loans."

Roger sits up in his chair and leans forward, "We didn't have a loan growth problem when I was CLO. Remember Don, we didn't have an Indirect Lending program either. I think we can grow our credit union without sacrificing our core values."

Sidney jumps in, "if I could spend $600 per member, like in Indirect, I bet Marketing could get members to *crawl* in off the street."

"What about those loan recapture programs", asks Kirkpatrick, "I'd rather give our own members $100 to refinance with the credit union than give $600 to a dealer for a loan to a stranger. Could we cut back on our Indirect program and run some recapture programs this next year? I hear

10

First United FCU is having tremendous success with their auto loan recapture program."

Beth nods her head in understanding and replies, "I think we should look at that, but we can't totally shut down Indirect." With a touch of sarcasm, she reminds everyone, "remember, where I'm from, every customer is a stranger. I have nothing against Indirect borrowers." The team laughs in response to her attempt to add humor to the discussion.

Roger tries to refocus the team by bringing them back to the subject of goal setting. "It seems to me that if our target is $500 million in assets and we currently have 24 thousand members and $470 million in assets, by my calculation we need to add about 1,500 members next year. Using an average of $19,500 in assets per member that is what it would take to get there."

"That sounds about right", Sydney says in agreement, "and that would be about $80 per member if we go with my $120,000 marketing initiative I'm proposing. That's a heck of a lot less than the $600 we're paying for Indirect auto loan members."

"So, if we go with this new marketing initiative, in addition to what we are already doing, and we focus on recapturing member auto loans instead of trying to squeeze profit out of Indirect, even if we don't hit our asset growth goal, we will still be better off financially", Roger concludes, "Because we are spending a lot less to acquire new members."

"But, what if we increase our assets, but our loan volume goes down?" Beth interjects, "We're going to have a tough time turning the ROAA we need if we are not making the loans."

Don jumps in again, to bring the discussion to a close, "I really like where we are headed here. It's really a different way of looking at things. But, we have been growing assets at 5% per year for the last five years, so if we just keep doing what we've been doing, we will naturally get really close to the $500 million mark, if not in December of next year, not long after. I'm just fearful that if we make the drastic changes that are being suggested, they may bite us in the butt! I'm not comfortable with that at all."

"Ok, so what you're saying is, let's make our goals to raise membership, deposit and lending by 5%", Roger summarizes, "are you agreeable to at least taking a stab at a loan recapture program?"

"Yes, certainly go ahead and give that a try. I'm not sure that it could hurt, and we may get some real traction with that", Mr. Kirkpatrick responds.

****

I realize the scenario above may sound like an over-simplification of a credit union leadership team planning session, and I may have drafted the worst-case scenario to man every position, but I'm sure you found something in this scenario that resonated with your own experience in similar meetings. As you read through the scenario, I bet you found some things that you agree with and some things that you don't agree with based on your own experience. You probably also noticed some data points that were used in each team members arguments. In fact, you may be satisfied that the members of this credit union leadership team were making data-driven decisions. But, I would like you to take a closer look.

The first thing we should look at is the goal to increase assets. Is it reasonable? I think it could be under the right circumstances. Certainly, asset size is important in many ways, and credit unions with more assets do have more flexibility to make large capital investments that smaller asset-sized credit unions do not. Executives can debate over its importance as a strategic goal and it is certainly true that a credit union half the size of another could be more profitable in absolute dollars as well as relative to assets. You could make an equally convincing argument, in some cases, that negative asset growth is just as important to the credit union to improve net worth ratios and ROAA, especially if the assets jettisoned are not performing well and a reduction in assets improves the credit union Net Worth Ratio. The key point here is that asset growth should be tied to a value outcome, other than size for size sake, which supports the credit unions mission and vision, and where there is data that supports the business decision to use asset growth as a goal. In this case, the CEO's desire to meet an arbitrary personal goal is not a good reason to use it.

Now, let's look at the $120 thousand marketing initiative. In this case, the V.P. of Marketing proposes the expenditure of *additional* marketing dollars for branding but provides no supporting data for why the additional dollars should be spent. In other words, the notion here is that spending more will yield increased results. In fact, when asked specifically, how many members the marketing campaign may generate, there is no response. To be fair, the V.P. was saved from having to answer that question because of Roger's opportunistic stab at criticizing a program that he didn't like, again with little data to support his assertions. Spending money should be related to a defined, desired outcome. 'X' number of dollars spent should be tied to an expected outcome value, 'Y', and 'Y' should correlate to a strategic goal.

Later in the discussion, the Marketing V.P. takes another stab at justifying the additional branding expense by pointing out that if the credit union is successful in attracting 1,600 new members to meet the asset growth goal, then the additional expense would only equate to $80 per member, much lower than Indirect dealer fees/incentives, or $600 per loan in this case. The trouble with this justification is that the COO/CFO estimate is that the credit union membership should increase by 1,600 in total, but experience tells us that 1,500 members per year will be added if they do nothing additional based on historic growth rates, so a goal of 1,600 is only 100 more than they would do with current expenditures. In effect, Sydney is looking to spend $1,200 for each additional new member added, above the average growth rate, which is twice as much as an Indirect loan costs to originate.

Roger is not a fan of Indirect lending and makes several comments about the programs ineffectiveness. While Mr. Baker's comments may be justified, he really provides no data to substantiate his claim. Beth is correct to point out that if the credit union's strategy is to grow loans and the Indirect lending program is generating the required amount of loans, then there needs to be some analysis done to determine whether Indirect loans can successfully be replaced by a direct recapture program. What happens, all too often, in the Indirect lending discussion is that the dealer participation fee, or incentive, is considered a loan cost and 100% charged against the loan cashflows. However, a dealer originated loan does not require the same level of direct marketing or internal processing that a direct loan requires. In most credit unions, marketing, origination, and servicing costs are not included in net yield measurements of loans originated directly by the credit union. So, it is not really a apples-to-apples comparison between Indirect loan and direct loan costs.

Additionally, there seems to be sentiment that Indirect lending borrowers are not good members, presumably because they do not open other deposit accounts and typically leave the credit union when their loan is repaid. This may be a valid point, but the hypothesis should be tested, and it should be determined whether that is true for all Indirect borrowers or just certain Indirect borrowers. Indirect lending can be very challenging, and many lenders simply do not take the time to conduct the proper analysis to maximize the potential benefit to the credit union and members. Purely relying upon anecdotal data can leave the credit union at a competitive disadvantage if one program or another is eliminated entirely. Remember, for any program you are willing to eliminate, there is another lender in the market that is willing to provide those services to your members.

Finally, Don closes the conversation by making a decision. His decision is basically based on his opinion after hearing everyone out. At the end of the conversation, Mr. Kirkpatrick has determined that the credit union will continue to do what it has been doing as it will likely get him to his personal goal, they are happy with their current financial performance, and making changes at this point may do more harm than good. This is called a HiPPO decision because it is based on the Highest Paid Persons Opinion. There is no doubt that the CEO is in charge and is ultimately accountable for his or her decisions, but the problem with this type of decision making is that it is very limiting. While the CEO's goal is to get to $500 million in assets, what if the credit union could hit $600 million is assets by doing things a little differently? What if the credit union is not serving as many members as it could because it is only pursuing low-risk auto loans? What if the credit union's current marketing efforts are not effectively attracting potential members? When data is not collected and analyzed, there are so many unanswered questions.

An organization with a data-driven decision culture behaves much differently than the hypothetical organization above. There are some key characteristics that can be found in an organization that uses data to inform business decisions:

> **Data Transformation Strategy** – a credit union with a data-driven culture has cultivated that culture using a defined organizational transformation strategy, rather than depending upon an organic emergence of data usage. The strategy should be based on a proper assessment of the current state, interviews with key

stakeholders in the organization, and provide short, medium, and long-term goals to ensure a complete transformation.

Leadership – leadership in the organization fosters the intentional use of data in decision making. Leaders avoid the temptation to drive decision-making based on experience and expertise alone. They insist on team members supporting decisions using relative data and analysis even if the results conflict with their opinions.

Access to Reliable Data – team members throughout the organization are provided unfettered access to enterprise data to use in decision making. Data is organized and managed in a way that provides a centralized, single source of the truth so that all decision-makers have access to the same data and the same language is used throughout the organization.

Data-Driven Team Members – people who are not accustomed to using data in decision-making find it difficult to transform to a data-driven decision culture without training. The organization invests in training existing team members, augmenting human resources with data analytics personnel and hire future employees who are trained and prepared to work in a data-driven decision culture. It is likely that some of the credit union's existing personnel will not be able make the transformation, but the credit union cannot be held back because of this resistance.

Data Augmented Decisions – an organization with a data-driven decision culture is making business decisions, daily, using data to support reasoning, is testing hypotheses to determine the best next action to take, and is evaluating performance to confirm decisions made.

****

Now, let's take another look at our organization above, but restacking the deck with data-driven team members. Here is what it might look like:

Don Kirkpatrick has been President/CEO of Hiawatha Hills Credit Union for the last ten years. The credit union has $470 million in assets and has seen 5%, year over year, asset growth for the past 5 years straight. Mr. Kirkpatrick has gathered his leadership team to discuss performance goals for the next year. Sidney Lane is the credit union's V.P. of Marketing and she has been with the credit union for four years. She came to HHCU from a smaller credit union in town where she was a Member Service Representative. Roger Baker is the credit unions CFO/COO. Roger was the Chief Lending Officer for the credit union before Don was promoted from the COO position to CEO, at which time Roger was promoted to CFO/COO. Finally, Beth Rogers is the Chief Lending Officer who joined the leadership team last year, having recently been the V.P. of Lending for a local community bank. Beth is the sixth CLO the credit union has had since Rogers promotion.

Kirkpatrick begins the meeting, "Well team, it's that time of year again. We need to set goals for the next year. As you all know, we established our Key Performance Indicators

18

last year, so I want to remind you that our goals should be relative to these measures: Net Income, Operating Costs to Income, Product Penetration, Market Share, and Member Satisfaction. Our research and analysis have shown that these measurements drive stable and balanced growth."

Ms. Lane responded, "We made noteworthy progress with product penetration over the past eighteen months; accounts per member is now 50% higher than the same size credit union in our area. We need to continue to tailor our product offerings to members based on predicted need/desire as our conversion rate on those offers are 100% higher than basic branding and generic product offerings."

"Congratulations on that, Sidney", says Roger, "Those marketing strategies have certainly stabilized membership growth and decreased attrition, even among those Indirect lending members who are so difficult to retain. 80% of those Indirect members used to abandon us when their loans were repaid. We have now reduced that attrition rate to less than 60%. It certainly makes Indirect Lending a more appealing option than it used to be."

"Yes, Roger, our focus on retaining those Indirect members has paid off, but we are doing a much better job of managing the network of dealers to better reflect our existing membership.", Beth responds, "While I think that Indirect Lending is still an excellent way to acquire new members, I should point out that we are still losing a significant number of member auto loan opportunities. Our research indicates that about 40% of existing members are still financing their vehicles purchases elsewhere. Based on our surveys, those decisions seem to be driven by dealer influence and we have been successful in recapturing about 25% of those loans that go to other dealers. I should point out that we have begun mining our Loan Origination System for potential members who were approved for a loan, but ultimately did not finance their purchase with us. I'm interested to see if we can convert these individuals."

Roger sits up in his chair and leans forward, "You know, the way we look at these measurements is a lot different than in the past. Don, remember when we used to sit around this table and pull numbers out of the air and argue about their significance? It seemed to work then, but the process we use today certainly seems a lot more refined and significantly less contentious."

Sidney jumps in, "I agree with Beth. Indirect continues to drive member growth and we have done a much better job of tailoring product offerings that better fit these members' needs. I do think we need to ramp up our recapture program to ensure that we are able to secure some of these relationships that we are currently losing. That said, we're going to need to increase deposits to cover our lending growth, so I'm recommending that we increase sales and marketing efforts on our deposit and investment products and services."

"Why wouldn't we use a recapture program in place of Indirect Lending", asks Kirkpatrick, "I'd rather give our own members $100 to refinance with the credit union than give $600 to a dealer for a loan to a stranger. Could we cut back on our Indirect program and use a recapture program exclusively this next year? I hear First United FCU is having tremendous success with their auto loan recapture program."

Beth nods her head in understanding and replies, "I agree with Sidney and think we should increase our use of that recapture program, but we can't totally shut down Indirect. While it seems that the cost to originate an Indirect Loan seems higher than the recapture program, there are two additional things to consider. One, we don't charge the cost of the recapture program against the loan as we do for Indirect origination costs so cost comparisons are not an equivalent, and two, the recapture program simply doesn't generate the volume of loans that Indirect does."

Roger tries to refocus the team by bringing them back to the subject of goal setting. "This is a very interesting conversation and it appears that we have some really positive things going on. How can we boil this discussion down into some goals? I'd like to see us continue to grow our loan portfolio, but we realize that attracting deposits will raise our cost of funds. We probably need to look at strategies for lowering the cost of loan originations and diversify our loan pricing to offset these additional costs."

"We are going to need to raise our deposit rates to be competitive", Sydney says in agreement, "we could conduct some A/B testing to see if our recapture program incentives could be adjusted. If we can lower the interest rate incentive and perhaps eliminate the gift card, that would provide significant savings. But, we would definitely need to test this hypothesis to see if works."

"We could certainly take on more risk in our loan portfolio to increase yields", Roger concludes, "70% of our loan portfolio is in our lowest risk tiers. Pricing in these tiers is just too low to generate the returns we are looking for. On the other hand, we do a really good job of mitigating the

21

risks of lower credit score borrowers. Our default rates are 50% of what is predicted by the credit bureau score."

"Yes, and I've been looking at ways to 'dynamically' price loans based on risk factors other than the credit score." Beth interjects, "We have found that a borrower with a 730 credit score and 120% loan-to-value ratio performs much worse than a borrower with a 730 credit score and a 70% loan-to-value. Today, these two borrowers get the same loan price based on their score. We want to change that so that loan pricing is more reflective of the actual risk."

Don jumps in again, to bring the discussion to a close, "I really like where we are headed here. It's really a different way of looking at things. The 'old' me wants to just set some high-level goals and head to the house, but we have found that using data to make better informed decisions about our goals has actually increased our member satisfaction ratings, because we are focusing on the things that matter to them, not us."

****

Hopefully, it was easy for you to see the difference in the latter example when compared to the previous. The first thing you should notice is that the President/CEO did not attempt to lead his team to set goals based on his opinion. Instead, he listened to his team and encouraged them when they used data to support their decision making. The second thing you should notice is that the leadership team had already established key statistics, known as KPI's, that they were using to measure success. They have previously determined that these measurements were most indicative of success toward a shared goal or value. Third, each member of the team had used data to make decisions related to their team but also integrated their decision making with the objectives of the entire credit union, not just their individual department success. Finally, you should notice the open and transparent discussion of data and goals. When data is accessible to the entire team, there is agreement on and confidence in its value. Time is not wasted debating the validity of the data.

Creating a data-driven decision culture doesn't mean that the credit union no longer treats its members as individuals. It's quite possible that data can provide insights about members that are not easily observed, and support tailored, individualized service offerings. Data-driven decision cultures are not about replacing human intuition but augmenting the human thought process to provide for more accuracy, confidence, and efficiency in the decision-making process. However, the transformation process isn't quick and easy and requires a structured and managed process. This book is intended to guide you and your credit union through the transformation process.

Chapter 2

My Personal Data Journey

I must admit, I might be a bit of a data geek. Not the type of data geek who pops up in the middle of a comedic movie scene and provides the exact chemical makeup of the moon's surface when someone says that the moon looks like a ball of cheese. I couldn't really care any less about that information because it is highly unlikely that it will ever have an impact on my life. However, in a political debate I am likely to provide you with the statistical probability of you being elected President of the U.S. based on whether you are right- or left-handed, although causation has never been established. In my defense, I have good reason to be so passionate about data. Data has come to my rescue on more than one occasion over the span of my career, but the very first time was almost thirty years ago. That said, I would describe myself as a social data geek. I'm passionate about data analytics but I can hold my own in a one-on-one conversation at the bar and not get thrown out.

When I was in my early twenties, I worked at a regional bank based in Columbus, OH. Our bank in Columbus was an affiliate of a larger bank holding company based in Cincinnati, where the "mothership" was located. I had recently been promoted to the collections department from my position as a teller and I found the work rewarding but challenging. It was good work for a young man and I was able to learn a lot about consumer lending at an early stage in my career. My first few months went well, and I received early praise for catching on to the collection process quickly, but then I started to receive criticism about the size of my account queue and my inability to successfully resolve delinquencies at the same rate as my two cohorts in the same department. I was confused and disheartened because I felt like I was doing my best every day, but the results were not measuring up.

Whenever I find myself in a position where I am potentially under-performing in comparison to peers, I begin to look for reasons why. Of course, I'm initially looking for areas where I may defend myself, but I am also looking for areas where I may be able to make improvements. In the above case, I began to think about possible explanations for the disparity in performance being reported by my manager. The first thing I considered was, what is the "proxy" measurement used to establish good and deficient performance? The second thing I considered was whether

25

the work was being evenly distributed among the team members? Finally, I wanted to consider whether the quality of borrowers was somehow different from one collector's queue to another's? Answers to these questions would certainly help me defend my position. But, they could also help me determine how I might improve my performance if all things were equal.

As to the measurement, in this case, the manager of the department was simply measuring the relationship between the number of accounts in a collector's queue at the beginning of the month to the number of accounts in the queue at the end of the month. Collector's with a higher positive difference were believed to be more effective. Mind you, accounts would fall delinquent (more than 30 days past due) throughout the month. A collections representative really had no control of the number of accounts that came into the queue after the first of the month, only the number of accounts that were brought current after they fell into the queue. In my case, there were months where the number of accounts in my queue at the end of the month wasn't much different than the number of accounts in my queue at the beginning of the month, relative to my cohorts. Based on the measurement used, I had done very little in that month.   Therefore, my manager's assessment was that I was not very successful improving the delinquency of accounts assigned to me. In fact, he once said, "You could have had a better impact on your queue if you hadn't shown up for work this month." Nice!

I then wanted to challenge whether the work load for each collector was equal and discovered that the way that the collections queues were divided was not altogether fair. In this case, we had three collectors working in our department and the manager had a bright idea to divide the letters of the alphabet by three and assign accounts by the first letter of borrowers' last name. There are 26 letters in the alphabet which results in 8.66 letters when divided by three. So, the manager counted letters, a, b, c, d, and so forth, until he reached 8.66 and then rounded up to nine. The first collector received the first nine letters, the second collector received the second nine letters and the third, well, the third only got eight letters. I was the first collector, so I got surnames that began with the letters "A" through "I", as in ice cream. I shouldn't have been too upset, as I was one of the two collectors with nine letters and there couldn't possibly have been a significant difference between the number of accounts held by the collectors who had nine letters and the collector who had only eight. So, the split seems even on the surface, right?

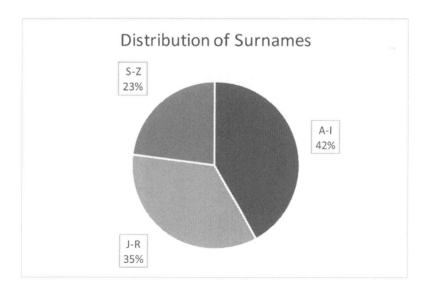

Wrong! The letters of the alphabet do not evenly distribute surnames in the U.S. If that were true, each letter would represent about 3.85% of the surnames in the population. In fact, over 10% of surnames in the U.S. start with the letter 'S' and less than 1% of surnames begin with the letter 'I', as in Icahn. If my bank's accounts were distributed based on actual percentages of surnames by first letter, then I was assigned 42% of the potential delinquent accounts, the second collector was assigned 35%, and the third collector was only assigned 23%. In other words, my potential work load was almost twice the work load of the collector assigned the latter third of the alphabet. Is it possible that a collector with half the workload of other collectors could be more effective in resolving delinquencies? The answer is, without a doubt, yes.

As to my third hypothesis, related to credit quality, it would have been extremely difficult to quantify at that time as we did not have access to credit scores, or any other risk score for that matter. Had we had access to a risk score, it would have been easy to measure the relative difference in credit quality from one segment of the portfolio to the other. None of this really mattered, as my fledgling avocation for using data analysis to fight my cause wouldn't have been accepted anyway. The fact was, in the mind of my manager at the time, I was an ineffective collector. The long-term effect of his opinion might have been my eventual termination or my voluntary departure out of frustration. In the short-term, it might have impacted opportunities within the bank that came my way or even annual salary increases. But, then something happened. Redemption came my way from a most unexpected source and I no longer had to hypothesize in isolation.

One morning, as I was going about my business "dialing for dollars", an unfamiliar individual showed up on the fourth floor of the Borden Building in downtown Columbus. This individual seemed to be someone with authority, but certainly wasn't from our local office. A striking female dressed in a dark suit and white blouse with a very large bow tied around the neck (it was the late eighties after all), she captured my attention for a moment and then disappeared into my managers office and shut the door behind her. After an hour or more, the office door came open and my manager walked straight to my desk.

"Mr. Cochrum", he said, "Can you come into my office?"

Of course, I was beside myself with instant worry as I rose from my desk and made my way to what was now becoming a very crowded office space. As I sat down, the woman, who I could barely glance at now, began,

"Mr. Cochrum, I am Mrs. Smith from the Cincinnati office."

My worry then became panic. She was from HQ!

"we have been monitoring collections activity here in the Columbus affiliate and we have found…"

For a minute, I think I lost consciousness. I was sure, based on the criticism I had received from my manager for three months straight, that day would be my last day in that job.

She continued, "we have found that, not only are you the most effective collector in the Columbus affiliate, you are the most effective collector in the entire system."

"Wait. What…, the what?", I responded either verbally or non-verbally, I can't remember.

"Yes", she persisted, "you have the highest number of payment promises per account assigned to you and the highest percentage of payments made because of a payment promise."

Now, there were measurements that I had never heard of or considered in my analysis, but that immediately made sense. In her measurement, it wasn't what I was assigned that mattered, which was out of my control, it was what I DID with what I was assigned that mattered. I learned that day that accurate measurements are important to good analytics and good analytics are important in making the right decisions about people and processes.

Nothing would delight me more than to tell you that I was promoted on the spot and that my fellow collectors picked me up and carried me down the corridor to my new corner office. Nothing like that happened. I didn't even get a blue ribbon to take home and share with my wife and kids, or a leg lamp at Christmas. What I received was the opportunity to keep working at the bank and higher expectations for performance. Such is life. But, I did walk away with a valuable education on the importance of good data and analytics that has led me through my entire work career.

Not to abruptly change domains, but this is the story of my data journey and, at this point, the trail heads in a new direction. For almost eight years, I was involved in ministry, sometimes while continuing to work in financial services and sometimes exclusively in ministry. Even in ministry, I found the opportunity to use data analytics to measure effectiveness. However, I can't say that my discoveries were always well received by my peers. This is how I learned my second lesson about analytics; analytics can tell us things that we don't want to hear. It is important to be careful how we use analytics to make our case. In the words of Colonel Jessup in the movie, *A Few Good Men*, some people "can't handle the truth!" Sometimes, the truth is evident but is not easy to accept in the moment. We need to be patient while others absorb the information that data reveals.

I served in an evangelical protestant church. It is important to understand for evangelicals there is no higher purpose than to "make disciples". It is referred to as being saved. My hypothesis was that modern-day evangelicals had lost their way and were focused on other things, not related to making disciples. This was in the mid-nineties when mega-churches were all the rage and church pastors were becoming celebrities in many ways. A lot of money was collected by churches from congregants and this money was often transformed into large physical campuses where members would congregate two or three times a week. One church, in the community where I lived, had a bowling alley in it. All very impressive, for sure, but was the activity translating into a growth in the number of people being saved? After all, making disciples is a biblical command for Christians, building churches with bowling alleys is not.

Embarking on this mission to measure effectiveness, I had to first decide on a proxy measure. A proxy measure is a measurement that is closely related to the outcome sought when direct measurements are not available. Increasing, or decreasing, the proxy has a direct effect on the outcome desired because they are highly correlated. In the credit union, product penetration measurements could be used as a proxy for member sentiment. Happy members consume more products, unhappy members close accounts. To measure the effectiveness of an evangelical church, baptisms could be used as a proxy for making disciples, as baptism is required by most evangelical churches as the immediate next step after being saved. Therefore, churches with more baptisms could potentially be more 'effective' than churches with fewer baptisms.

This measurement isn't quite fair in isolation, as church size must have something to do with productivity. More church members should equate to more baptisms and larger churches should, theoretically, have more baptisms. But that was not exactly what I was trying to prove. I was trying to make the case that money was not effectively being used to support the ultimate purpose of the churches' existence. I wanted to find out how much it 'cost' to spread the gospel and make disciples. In business, we compare input to output to determine efficiency. Therefore, I would compare church expenditures to baptisms to determine individual church efficiency. Were the investments made yielding the results desired?

Since the case that many churches made, at that time, about the use of money on extravagance was that it was being used to "equip" church members to make disciples, I wanted to know just how much it cost to baptize one person. Presumably, churches spending more money per member were providing higher levels of equipment which should result in higher levels of effectiveness. So, I gathered information from churches across my county and did the math. I found that churches spent, on average, $22,000 for every person baptized in the church the previous year. Some churches were much lower and some much higher, but the size of the church made little difference. Large congregations were just as effective, or ineffective if you will, as small churches. Some of the smallest churches were more effective than the mega-churches. My ultimate argument was, couldn't we be more effective in meeting our goal if we stopped building churches and filling them with people and simply hired people to go around making disciples full-time? It's kind of an inside sales vs. outside sales thing. My point wasn't to close churches but merely to point out that that there was a need for a higher level of effectiveness.

As I said previously, this was not a popular argument to make among evangelicals at the time. The response I received most often was, "It doesn't matter how much money is spent, as long as one soul is saved!" I suppose that is true at a foundational level, but when that money is being wasted on prideful creature comforts instead of putting boots on the ground, I think one would be justified in arguing that it does matter after all. I didn't bring it up much again after my original analysis, but it is interesting what a couple of decades have proven out.

In recent years, churches have decided that people don't respond as well to the mega-church with its large campuses, glitz, and glamour[4]. Many churches are being formed today in small venues and when they grow to a certain size, they branch off into a new, smaller church. In general, churches are collecting and spending far less money today than they did in the past. Millennial evangelicals seem to be pursuing more authenticity and practicality than creature comforts and entertainment. Was I right? Who knows? But, I did do the analysis and one can say that the data told an interesting, if not prescient, story.

So, let me return my focus to financial services as I did in 1999 when I entered the credit union movement by way of a small Dallas, Texas-area credit union. To make this segue work, allow me to point out the philosophical similarities between churches and credit unions that I immediately recognized that made credit unions different from the banks I had worked for in the past. While their business models are much different, the importance and status of the 'member' is equal among churches and credit unions. Credit unions and churches both love to count members, even if those members participate very little within the organization. The 'conversion' of a member, if you will, is tantamount to winning the argument, for churches between good and evil and for credit unions, well, also between good and evil. Credit union leaders and church

---

[4] https://www.crosswalk.com/church/pastors-or-leadership/5-reasons-your-church-should-be-smaller.html

leaders are generally people-oriented rather than process-oriented. In the same way that churches believe that there is no amount of money considered too much to save a lost soul, credit unions can exert a disproportionate amount of effort and resources to meet a single member's needs. Credit unions typically have higher operating costs than their banking counterparts. Both have historically found little value in data to inform what they do and rely mostly on intuition to make decisions about their organizations. So, in many ways, the credit union environment felt very familiar to me in my mid-career transition from fulltime ministry back into financial services.

In contrast, banks and finance companies consider consumption more highly than interaction. In other words, there are customers that banks and finance companies are willing to ignore because they don't fit their business model and do not consume their products and services. In the interest of efficiency, for-profit financial institutions are willing to ignore people on the fringe. Banks and finance companies are willing to sacrifice an individual customer's experience to appease a face-less, disassociated stockholder. For-profits are extremely process oriented, looking for the most efficient way to complete a process which, in turn, yields potentially higher profits, but leaves some customers empty-handed.

As with all things, neither philosophy is all good or all bad. However, one does have to step back and, in a moment of self-criticism, ask why it is, if credit unions are the best choice for consumers, why so many consumers choose banks over credit unions? You might be tempted to say it's because banks have better name recognition and people don't really understand what a 'credit union' is. But, whose fault is that? Others may say that they don't want to do business the way banks do, just to grow. But, the question is, do we know these things to be true, based on data? Or, are these the explanations that we have grown comfortable with over time because we believe in what we are doing so passionately and fail to take a critical look at our products, people and processes?

Allow me to return briefly to my days in ministry, once again. At one point in my experience in church leadership, I found that people were not attending Sunday morning bible study classes as they once did. These classes were small groups held prior to the morning worship service, often referred to as Sunday School. Many of the experts of the day were prepared to say that people just don't want to come to Sunday School anymore. "Times are changing", they would say. It would have been easy for me to accept this explanation because promoting and staffing those activities with volunteers was exhausting and I could willingly give that up. But, I wasn't willing to accept the premise, so I hired a church growth consultant to come in and provide some guidance.

The consultant gave me some homework to do, which basically was a survey asking me what consistent efforts were being made by our church to support growth in attendance in our Sunday School classes. I didn't get halfway through the survey before I realized, it wasn't that Sunday School didn't work, it was that we had stopped working Sunday School. In other words, we had taken for granted that Sunday School was a critical part of the church experience and that people would continue to come despite any effort or lack of effort made. We may be guilty, within the credit union movement, of believing our mantra that credit unions are simply better for consumers without quantifying what that means using data. In other words, can and should consumers find value in our credit union beyond our simple belief that we are a better option for them?

You have probably read that credit union asset growth continues, which indicates that credit unions are growing. Growing businesses are good. However, what isn't often reported along-side asset growth is market share. Credit union market share has remained relatively flat over the past ten years and oscillates between 5% and 7.5%[5]. Small banks and thrifts are continually being absorbed by larger banks which now command 73% of the market. There are a lot of things at play in these statistics, but the overwhelming truth is that the current rate of change within the credit union movement isn't yet enough to make a significant impact on the consumer market. If you've guessed that I will eventually get to the point of claiming that data analytics may be part of the answer, you are correct, but we can continue this discussion later. I just wanted to wrap this segment up by suggesting that the current credit union leadership philosophy might need to be tweaked a bit to affect change. We may want to test some of our long-held beliefs about member value using data and analytics to see if we can better meet the demands of today's consumer.

I think that I may have been one of the first people in the credit union space to speak publicly about the importance of data analytics and business intelligence, starting back in 2010. There are certainly a lot of

---

[5] https://www.philadelphiafed.org/-/media/research-and-data/publications/banking-trends/2017/bt-credit_unions.pdf?la=en

people talking about it today. Publicly, my emphasis has been on loan portfolio management and risk; however, my work with credit union data proceeded my work specifically in the lending field. My initial work in the credit union space was in marketing and business development. I began my work in a small but well-placed credit union in the DFW Metroplex. I had the perfect vantage point for learning all aspects of the credit union business while also gaining an understanding of the politics and core values of the credit union movement.

One of my first recollections as a Marketing Director at the credit union was my responsibility for creating statement stuffers that went out with each monthly statement. I have evidence that this part of my job was inconsequential, but that is not the point of this story. This story is about a particular month in which I was stumped about what to feature on the current month's promotional statement stuffer. I went to the CEO of the credit union for advice. Her response to me was that the credit union typically ran a CD promotion this time of the year, every year. Simple enough, I thought, but didn't I also hear that our deposits were currently too high? Our loan ratio was too low, so why would we promote more, long-term deposits? What did I know, I was a marketing person, not a finance person? None of that mattered. What mattered is what we had always done. Our members got a CD promotion that month and the promotion had little impact on deposits because the current rates were too low.

Now, it's not my argument that I was smarter than everyone else. My point is that our actions as a credit union did not seem to coincide with reality. We seemed to be more focused on our expectations of how members should have behaved or how they expected us to behave from a traditional sense (what did we do last year?) than doing things that were beneficial to our members or met a perceived need. Another case in point, we had one of the lowest NSF fees in the region. We only charged members $10 if they overdrew their checking account. You can certainly argue that is a huge benefit to members that consistently overdraw their accounts. But, on the other hand, we only had one poorly placed ATM in the Metroplex, and members who tried to access their accounts near where they lived or shopped were charged transaction fees. In other words, the problem, as I surmised, was that our financially responsible members were subsidizing those who overdrew their accounts by paying foreign ATM transaction fees. This had a direct impact on our ability to attract new members as other financial institutions were offering free ATM transactions. This is, of course, important to a marketing director, as it created a competitive disadvantage.

So, I did an analysis and found that we could raise our overdraft fee to $35 and waive all foreign ATM transaction fees. The fee-structure change would balance out, according to my analysis. You must be careful, of course, to keep in mind that this is not a zero-sum game. Obviously, if one raises the NSF then there will likely be fewer instances of overdrafts and if you lower foreign transactions fees, there will be more foreign transactions. You simply need to make some assumptions on what the impact of such a change might be, or conduct A/B testing with a small group of members. But the overarching premise was, no one is going to choose not to open a checking account with us because the overdraft fees are too high. Who asks about overdraft fees when opening a checking account? On the other hand, waiving foreign transaction fees overcomes a huge objection to those who want to do business with us. One could offset the other, but only analysis can prove it to be true.

My final argument based on my journey's experience: Several credit unions I have worked with are very focused on providing a positive experience for all members, even those that you could reasonably argue haven't earned it. This holds true in consumer lending automation, for example. Most non-credit unions have nearly automated the entire lending decision process, because doing so can significantly lower costs of loan originations. Lenders purchase Loan Origination Software (LOS) that can make automated lending decisions and facilitate the loan closing process. However, most credit unions essentially turn off the automated decision engine in lieu of having each application underwritten by a human underwriter. Even those that do allow some automated decisions typically refuse to allow a member to be declined by "the system". This is all falls under a premise that we don't want to miss an opportunity to help a member in need.

However, in a former position I held with a lending software company, I did a study which showed that indirect auto loan applications that were rendered an approval by an LOS were 50% more likely to fund than those applications that were manually approved. And, the longer the underwriting process takes, the less likely an approval of any kind would be funded. In other words, the credit union could serve 50% more members if the credit union were to render more automated approval decisions or could even render manual approvals faster. Automated decisions on 'no-brainer' applications allow human underwriters to focus their work on the truly difficult decisions, turning their decisions around faster. An LOS, if properly implemented, can improve efficiency, and dramatically improve the member experience of those you are most likely to serve.[6]

These improvements require some level of data analysis; they can't simply be based on intuition. In some engagements with credit unions, I found loans that were referred for underwriting when a specific decision rule was violated, and about 98% of the time, a human underwriter ultimately declined the application. In those cases, it makes little sense for highly qualified lenders to play loan application "Whack-a-Mole", opening applications to simply click the decline button. We must allow technology to do the work so that we can spend our time on members who qualify for our low-cost products and services.

My data journey has brought me to a place where I am passionate about helping credit unions help their members and make a larger impact in the financial services industry. I believe data analytics and business intelligence is one way of doing that. Many studies have shown that management decisions based on sound analytics can be more accurate and provide more consistent results than intuitive decisions based on assumptions and experience. Financial Services disruptors are having a

---

[6] http://www.cutoday.info

significant impact on consumer financial products as they start with the technology and point it at a problem rather than starting with a problem and looking for technology to solve it. It is my desire to help credit unions become what they should be, the most effective and attractive financial service provider for the average consumer.

Chapter 3

The Case for Data-Driven Decision Transformation

W. Edwards Deming is claimed to have said, "Without data, you are just another person with an opinion." Mr. Deming has often been overlooked as a data analytics thought-leader in the U.S., because most of his recognizable work, before the nineteen-seventies, was done overseas, in Japan. He is recognized with a TQM award named in his honor, The Deming Prize, for being responsible for the relatively rapid growth of Japanese industry between 1950 and 1960[7]. Much of his work was not well known in the U.S. until well after his work was completed in Japan. Deming's work in manufacturing efficiency and quality was based on the notion that improvements in quality could be made in studying data and making incremental improvements towards the goal of perfection. What the Japanese discovered, now almost seventy years ago via Deming's tutelage, is that management decisions made, absent reliable and accurate data, are no better than one man's guess over another's.

---

[7] The Essential Deming: Leadership Principles from the Father of Quality

Think for a minute about how your credit union develops lending policy and procedure today. We look at defaulted loans that yield a loss and observe commonalities between those loans. Then we write a policy or procedure to mitigate the impact of that common attribute. For example, let's say five out of ten of the credit union's latest auto loan defaults had the common characteristic of having a debt-to-income (DTI) ratio greater than 40%. Our tendency is to enhance or policies or procedures or construct new policies and procedures with the intent to eliminate the possibility of loans with high DTI ratios from defaulting in the future. In this case, our new guideline would state that a borrower's DTI could not exceed 40%. But this new guideline has only taken the defaulted loans into consideration, not all of the other loans in the portfolio with DTI's higher than 40% that are still performing well. This usually results in fewer loans being originated, potentially both good and bad.

The issue with improvement by elimination is that it is not an innovative approach, doesn't lead to gained efficiency and makes it difficult to improve the quality of service offered to our members because it adds constraints. In fact, taking drastic measures to eliminate risk makes it virtually impossible to expand product and service offerings to members who need them. In almost every credit union that I have worked with, there is at least one loan product the credit union will not offer its members. For many years, credit unions would not offer Indirect auto loans, or point of sale lending because the perceived risks were too high. Other credit unions have stopped offering recreational vehicle loans or motorcycle loans, for example. There is usually a story explaining why they no longer offer these loans to their members and those stories are usually focused on the loans that went bad, not the loans that performed well. Think about it this way, while you may have taken a large loss on a few loans, there were still a lot of loans that didn't default and didn't cause a loss. When the credit union eliminates products or services offered, with broad strokes, it not only eliminates the potential of non-performance, it also eliminates the potential for high performing loans.

Henny Youngman, a stand-up comedian popular in the mid-twentieth century once joked[8], "Doctor, it hurts when I do this." The doctor responds, "Then don't do that." In many ways, the risk mitigation strategy above is not unlike this doctor's advice. We wouldn't accept this kind of advice from a doctor without a formal and extensive evaluation, so why would we accept the same kind of decision-making in our credit union, simply stopping what doesn't work without exploring ways of making things work better. Edwards Deming would suggest to us that a study of process and performance data would lead us to better conclusions as to how we should change our policies, guidelines, and procedures to support better performance in the future.

So, the journey begins. As with any journey, a credit union's transformation to data-driven decisions has an origin and a destination. It is important to understand the journey and what should be expected as it will prevent the temptation to quit or turn back to old decision-making

---

[8] http://www.funny2.com/henny.htm

methods when the journey becomes difficult. For now, let's start at the origination point.

Referring to Deming's statement above on opinions, what are some of the opinions you have heard among your credit union's leadership that describe the reasons why the credit union has been unable to achieve growth or improved performance? In my work with credit union across the country, there are several opinions that I've heard on a few occasions:

- Our Members appreciate the human touch. That is why we are not interested in process automation.

- Our auto loan recapture program is the best way to generate member auto loans.

- We can't afford data analytics in our credit union.

- Members who apply for loans online are willing to wait for an answer.

- I can't trust credit scores.

These are actual opinions shared with me by credit union executives, and I've heard many more. As one can see, these opinions run the gamut and may be shared by other credit unions nationwide. But, they are just opinions. There is little data to confirm or dispel them. In fact, there may be overwhelming data to prove that the opposite is true in every case. I will address these specific opinions at the end of this chapter and provide some insight into how one might derive a hypothesis from these opinions and then test them to ascertain whether they can be confirmed. But, for now, this is where most credit unions will originate their transformational journey.

What does it mean to create a data-driven decision culture in your credit union? Simply defined, a data-driven decision culture is one in which the credit union is equipping and training employees to make decisions using data, while fostering a culture that acts on data rather than solely on intuition. It is important, however, to also define the difference between data-driven and intuition as many will argue that the experience that informs their intuition also constitutes data. When I refer to data in this context, I am referring to measurements used in statistical analysis where processes are used to validate the significance of the measurements observed. It is much more than saying, "I've seen something that looks like this before." This doesn't discount the value of experience and intuition because domain experience is essential for determining whether measurements are relevant to the business, but it does recognize the potential pitfalls associated with solely using our intuition.

Now, if you are like most people, you rely on your intuition quite often. In fact, intuition is part of the mental process where your brain can use learning to shortcut decision-making. In his book, *Thinking, Fast and Slow*, Daniel Kahneman describes our intuition as the process used in our brain to respond fast, or quickly, to questions. The mental process that deliberates on facts and new information is considered the slower process. If you think back to when you learned to drive a car, you often over-steered or under-steered, over-accelerated and over-braked. This is because your brain had to thoughtfully consider every move, because the experience was new to you. As you gained experience, your reactions became more fluid. In fact, while it is not advisable, experienced drivers can often successfully navigate familiar routes while 'multi-tasking'. This is because their brain is operating on 'auto-pilot', or intuition. Accidents typically occur when unexpected events happen, and your brain is required to shift from the faster, intuitive process to the slower, deliberative process. Often, there is not enough time to make that shift in time to avoid disaster.

This can be true of business decisions, too. While our intuition can effectively help us speed up the decision-making process in everyday, routine activities, scientific studies have proven that our intuition is prone to error when used in more complex decision making. Scientists refer to the root cause of these errors as Cognitive Bias and we are all susceptible to them. Here are the top five cognitive biases:

Availability Heuristic (This just happened) – This often occurs when we rely heavily on recently obtained information to confirm our hypothesis. In everyday life, you may hear a new song by a band you've never heard of. Then for the next two days you keep hearing other songs by this same band. These songs had always been played, but you only recently made the association between the songs and the band, so you become more aware of the playing of the songs by that specific band. An example of how this could happen in the credit union can be found in the lending department. Let's say over the last three months, three out of seven vehicles repossessed were BMW 3-Series automobiles, all financed from one dealer. A common response to this observation would be to either discontinue financing BMW 3-Series automobiles, discontinue financing vehicles for the dealership in question, or both. But, this could possibly be an error and making such a decision could put the credit union at a competitive disadvantage. What if, for example, BMW automobiles make up a high percentage of the vehicles financed by loans in your auto loan portfolio. It would make sense that a higher percentage of repos would also be BMW automobiles. The same is true for the dealer in question. If that dealer is a high-volume dealer then it is likely that a higher number of their vehicle loans will be represented in your auto loan portfolio. The test to eliminate this bias would be to conduct a statistical analysis of all loans in your loan portfolio and determine whether the repo rate of this collateral from this dealer was statistically significant when compared to all loans in the portfolio over time.

Salience Error (It would be awful if that happened) - This occurs when statistically irrelevant information is used in the decision process that purports significance, typically based on fear. Consider these two scenarios. In the first scenario, a borrow requests a $17,200 loan to purchase a $19,000 recreational vehicle. The borrower's income supports the payments and the value of the collateral is equal to the purchase price, or $19,000. If the borrower has a good credit score, we can agree that it is likely that this loan is going to be approved. In the second scenario, the borrower would like $80,000 to purchase a $100,000 recreational vehicle. Again, the borrower's income can support the payments, the collateral value is equal to the purchase price and the borrower has a good credit score. It is likely that, because of the amount of the loan, there is a higher probability that we would not agree to do this loan. In fact, this is true in many credit union environments and the reasoning is nothing more than the loan amount and the *fear* of the potential single loss. Nobody wants to have their name associated with a loss that large.

We can obviously come up with a number of bad things that could happen, but the point is that these decisions are not based on a comparison of actual data related to the performance of similar loans but on the size of the potential loss if something goes wrong without determining that the size of the loan, in and of itself, poses a higher risk. This is an example of Salience Error.

Ostrich Effect (This can never happen) – Can anyone say mortgage lending? This error is based on the false belief that whatever is suggested could not happen for several reasons. Your decision is a sure bet. I recall, six years ago, making a presentation at the CUNA Lending Conference in Miami. At the time, several credit unions were investing in pools of medallion loans. These are loans made to owners of taxi cab licenses in major metropolitan areas, like New York City. They were believed to be a low-risk investment because the value of the collateral was stable and rising, and these major cities were not issuing new medallions, thereby protecting collateral demand. In my presentation, I suggested that it was a fallacy to assume, as many had done, that because there had never been an issue with these loans that there would never be an issue with them.

After my presentation was completed, a member of the lending council pulled me aside and suggested that I take the comments related to medallion lending out of my presentation. He claimed that he had fully studied the risks associated with medallion lending and he was confident that the risks were low, or even non-existent. He insinuated that my comments were careless and not well thought-out. I re-iterated my point in the presentation which was, anytime money leaves the credit union there is a risk of it not coming back. Those risks need to be considered. In fact, the Medallion Financial Corporation, the country's largest medallion lender, references a number specific risks associated with medallion lending in its annual report.

When I made my presentation in 2012, while already launched in Manhattan[9], Uber was not even a blip on the transportation radar and had not had a significant impact on the transportation market. Neither I, nor anyone else in the audience in Miami, could have known the impact Uber would have on the taxi business. By 2014, taxi cab competition, like Uber, had impacted medallions so significantly (76% decline in value)[10] that the NCUA issued a letter to credit unions providing guidance as to how the credit union should evaluate the specific risks of medallion loans[11].

In 2018, two east coast credit unions, Melrose and LOMTO, were closed due to significant medallion loan losses. A third, Progressive, is on the ropes[12] as I write this chapter. I don't get many opportunities to say this,

[9] https://www.businessinsider.com/ubers-history#august-2013-uber-moves-into-india-and-africa-and-it-closes-a-series-c-funding-round-that-sees-an-enormous-258-million-investment-from-google-ventures-this-round-values-uber-at-376-billion-15

[10] https://www.claconnect.com/resources/articles/2017/taxi-medallion-loans-lose-value-burdening-financial-institutions

[11] https://www.ncua.gov/Resources/Documents/SupervisoryLetter_TaxiMedallion.pdf

[12] http://www.cutoday.info/Fresh-Today/Declining-Taxi-Medallion-Values-Continue-

but I was right on this one. Does it offend me that my words of caution were ignored? No, it saddens me when credit unions make errors like this that could be avoided. This is an example of the Ostrich Effect; ignoring relevant facts that contradict one's intuition.

The Outcome Bias (That has never happened) – this bias looks similar to the previous one, but in this case the risk may be recognized but is dismissed because it has never actually happened. Many young managers suffer from Outcome Bias. We call it throwing caution to the wind, but we will see people with little experience ignore caution because the potential negative outcomes have never happened to them. They got away with it, if you will. This bias also fosters fraud, because we tend to not consider risks that we have never confronted, and fraudsters capitalize on our complacency to these risks. A Dallas area credit union was once the victim of millions of dollars in fraudulent loans when it was discovered that tax returns had been falsified. The funding personnel were not validating tax return information with random audits and a ring of members had learned to falsify these documents in order to inflate income. The credit union had never seen an instance of fraudulent tax returns, so there were no procedures for validating the authenticity of these documents.

This becomes an issue when a credit union relies heavily on the past behavior of a specific member, for example, or employee to make a decision about a current risk. The notion is, since this member has never defaulted in the past, it is highly unlikely that they will default in the future, despite what current risk measurements indicate. Because an employee has previously acted with integrity, they will always act with integrity. While it can be risky to allow a member to become over-extended or give an employee too much discretion, it can also lend itself to fraud as a member gains the confidence of the lender or an employee gains the confidence of their manager, and then uses the familiarity of the relationship to take advantage of the credit union. It has also been an issue for some credit unions in the Indirect lending business. As dealer personnel, outside the credit union, become more familiar with credit union representatives, they attempt to leverage that relationship to request special favors. They may say, "You know I've always sent you good business. I need this one favor and I promise, you won't be sorry." When we assume something will not happen because it has not happened, we fall victim to Outcome Bias.

Confirmation Bias (I knew that will happen) Confirmation bias is when we focus on information that only supports our preconceived determination, ignoring information that is contradictory. I've analyzed a number of credit union loan portfolios and I've observed, time and time again, that the presence of a qualified co-borrower can significantly reduce the risk of default, in some cases as much as 66%. But when I ask lenders what they consider the value of a co-borrower to be, they often state that the presence of a second borrower is insignificant. Then I show them the supporting data that proves that, although co-borrowers on defaulted loans are typically unreliable, loans with two borrowers default significantly less often than loans with single borrowers, which suggest that there should be a pricing differential in a risk-based pricing environment. My argument rarely changes the lender's mind because they are convinced that co-borrowers have negligible effect on recovering losses on defaulted loans. Every loan that defaults with a co-borrower confirms their hypothesis.

****

Like many who have attended my seminars, you may be stuck at this point. You may believe that data can be helpful in decision making, but you still trust your gut more than your computer. I like to ask seminar attendees whether they think that humans make better decisions than computers do. Invariably, at the beginning of the discussion, most attendees agree that humans make better decisions. While it is true that human beings are better at reasoning than computers, scientific studies have proven, over and over again, that computers make more consistent decisions over time than humans.

For those that are still convinced that humans are better decision-makers, I remind them that if they took a flight to the conference where I am speaking, 95% of that flight was managed by a computer. The reason for that is that crash data has proven that most airline accidents are caused by human error and the more of a flight that a computer can handle, the lower the probability of a crash. Three of the top five causes of airliner accidents are attributable to human error or human related causes. It is not clear that the two remaining reasons could be significantly improved with human interaction. Finally, most all the automotive innovations we have seen in the last decade have been technologies designed to prevent accidents caused by driver error. To move beyond intuitive decision making, where many credit unions are today, you must agree that there is a significant benefit to data-driven decision making.

****

Common Opinion Arguments

Automation vs. Human Contact

Automation does seem impersonal at the outset when describing any process that was initially performed by a human and has been translated into a mechanized or automated process. Automation also poses the potential loss of control which humans may currently possess in a process. Take, for instance, the Automated Teller Machine (ATM) which was first introduced in 1969[13]. Prior to the introduction of the ATM, a banking customer would go to the bank, wait for a teller, and request a withdrawal of cash from their account. The teller would verify available funds in a depositors account and then dispense cash as appropriate. But, the first ATMs were 'offline', not connected to a network, and there was a potential that an account owner would attempt to withdrawal more money from their account than was available. One might have argued that this risk was unacceptable and shut down the project, but instead, banks at the time decided that each account owner would be given a daily withdrawal limit that seemed tolerable to the financial institution and the depositor. Of course, in addition to the risk argument above, many bankers argued

---

[13] https://www.wired.com/2010/09/0902first-us-atm/

that their customers would not take to these machines and would prefer to transact with a live teller. On this point, they were, at least, partially right.

The fact is, that while financial institutions had hoped that ATMs would make costly branches obsolete, this result has not significantly materialized, primarily because the technology did not exist for ATMs to provide the level of service that human tellers could. But, I've never heard a financial institution suggest to me that they were going to eliminate ATMs, except in specific places where there was little use. The fact is that ATMs have found their place in the financial services industry, but they have not entirely replaced human tellers at this point. What this proves is there are no absolutes when it comes to credit union member sentiment. We can never say that all our members prefer one thing or another. It is probably truer that for any technology innovation in financial services there will be a transformation of the member over time, with growing acceptance correlated with value which we will discuss below. Anecdotally, I can say that I prefer as much automation as my credit union can throw at me with the option of choosing human interaction if needs be.

On the other hand, I've seen the opposite approach taken by some credit unions, which is to assume that all members are ready to embrace automation. Recently, my own credit union chose to replace all its in-branch tellers with Interactive Teller Machines (ITMs). It is obvious that someone told them to use the band-aid approach to change. The band-aid approach is where you rip the band-aid off a wound and take all the pain at one time, rather than over an extended period. From what I observed, the

56

pain on the first few days after this change was intense for the credit union. Anecdotally, I have heard that several members, who use the same local branch, have fled to other nearby financial institutions, primary due to the chaos created by this change.

The concept of the ITM is to have centralized human teller resources that interact with members remotely through ATM-like technology in the branch. Obviously, a financial institution might choose this strategy where human tellers assigned to a branch were not utilized effectively and where aggregating those resources in a centralized location would add more efficiency. But, the roll out of this technology, which I was excited about, was an initial disaster. Where I previously rarely waited for a live teller in the branch, I now found myself waiting for an open ITM and, once successfully gaining access to a machine, waiting for a live teller at a remote location to become available. All I wanted to do is make a loan payment and verify the payment amount.

It should be argued by credit union leaders that members will prefer value over automation, or the human touch. In other words, if automation creates a greater value for the member, it will probably be preferred over the human touch. If all the value gains from automation are going to the financial institution, then members will be slower to embrace a shift to higher levels of automation. Automation should never subtract value from the member. If value is provided by the human touch and not by technology, then the member will, in fact, appreciate the human touch over automation, and vice versa. If the credit union is seeking to improve efficiencies and lower costs, then the credit union must also offer a value to the member for adopting change. The question isn't really between the human touch or automation, it is really about value. Proper testing and data analytics help establish perceived values and support making changes that benefit the credit union and the member alike.

The proper, and perhaps wiser, way to implement a transition to automation is to begin with an A/B testing process. Instead of assuming a zero-sum game in calculating the cost savings of automation, the credit union should conduct testing in different scenarios to observe the impact to the member and potential hidden or unexpected costs of change, before making the change enterprise-wide. When A/B testing is used, the credit union can document questions that they didn't initially have when considering a change. Then, they can work to answer those questions and retest. Here is an example from my experience during my own credit union's transition that could have made things go much better.

My first interaction with the ITM was to deposit a check into my business account from a client credit union. I approached the ITM, prepared to, perhaps, type in my account number and make the deposit. Instead, I had to wait for the remote teller to join me at the machine. She then asked me to enter my account number and then initiated the process for the machine to accept my check. She reviewed the check and then provided me my receipt. My argument is that if this process had been tested in advance, decision-makers would have determined that with this type of transaction, there is no need for a remote teller to be present. This is probably true for 85% of transactions handled by an ITM. I would even argue that if it was determined that a live teller HAD to review the deposit, most of the work could have been done by me while waiting for the teller and then the wait would have only been for the teller to verify my work. Now, before you ask yourself why I didn't use remote deposit, let me just say that is a whole other issue.

Finally, on this topic, consumers have proven to embrace good and valuable automation. However, bad automation is never acceptable. Instead of assuming all members seek the human touch, the credit union should test that hypothesis before making a final decision. Not doing so, can put the credit union far behind its competitors as automation makes gains in the financial services sector.

Auto Loan Recapture Programs

In a previous life, I spent a considerable amount of time helping credit unions create and manage Indirect auto lending programs, where members finance their auto purchases with loans originated at the dealership or point of sale. In these types of transactions, the dealer, or merchant, originates the loan and sells it to the lender for a fee. This origination fee, or participation, can be a considerable amount which will take the lender several months to recoup in interest charges. Many credit unions have opted out of this type of relationship with dealers for a few reasons, but one of the biggest reasons is the upfront origination cost.

According to the National Auto Dealers Association, 70% of auto buyers choose to finance their purchase at the dealership selling the vehicle. This includes, in many cases, credit union members. If the credit union does not have a point-of-sale agreement with the dealer where their members buy a vehicle, it is likely that the credit union will not finance the purchase of the vehicle at the outset. This is not up for debate. However, there are marketing programs that attempt to identify members who recently purchased and financed automobiles with other lenders. Once these members are identified, they are prompted to refinance their purchase with the credit union with a low rate offer and cash incentive. Case in point: the last time I purchased a vehicle, I was offered 50 basis points off the rate charged by the dealer captive lender and promised a $100 gift card to refinance with my credit union. I was on that deal like a hound dog on table scraps. But, is this arrangement ultimately good for the credit union and the member?

Analysis of the Hypothesis

Costs	Indirect	Recapture
Origination Cost	$500	$100
Total Interest Revenue Over 30 Months	$2,170	$1,910
Net Income over 30 Months	$1,670	$1,810
Difference		$140

Above is a quick analysis of the hypothesis that an auto loan recapture program is better than an Indirect auto lending program based only on the transaction values. In this analysis, it is assumed that the loan amount is $25,000 financed over 72 months at 4.25% and an average loan life of 30 months (the average loan repays in 30 months instead of 72 months). It also assumes that the lender pays the dealer 2% of the loan amount to originate the loan in the Indirect program. This analysis does not include the cost to manage either program, but for simplicity, let's say at this point that it is equal. As one can see, using the assumptions above, the recapture program is less expensive than the Indirect program, by $140 per loan. But, is it more convenient for the member?

However, If the credit union lowers its dealer incentive to 1% of the loan amount, suddenly, the Indirect program becomes $110 less expensive on a per loan basis. Other questions not answered by this analysis but easily analyzed through A/B testing are, can the credit union originate MORE loans using the recapture program or LESS, and what is the member preference? Because the difference in one program and the other is manageable to the point of making them of equal value, member sentiment and volume become significant questions that need to be answered.

We can't afford data analytics in our credit union

On the surface, it is difficult to determine how this hypothesis could be tested. However, at least two ideas come to my mind. The first is take a single process in the credit union and conduct a test to determine whether there is opportunity for improvements that reduce costs or increase revenue. If a small-scale test demonstrates that data analysis can add to the bottom line, then one can extrapolate those savings across several processes or products to determine potential value. The second way to prove or disprove this hypothesis is to compare financial institutions that have invested in data analytics and those that have not. If those that have invested in data analytics show significant increases in ROI, then one can make the case that the credit union should invest more in data analytics. However, there is an argument that could be made that better performing organization use analytics because they are better at performing analytics rather than saying that analytics makes them a better performing organization. This is a correlation vs. causation argument.

Having said that, I think the premise is faulty, as it is not clear how one would determine the 'cost' of analytics. Some analytics could add little to no cost. A data-driven culture is a way of thinking and behaving. While the reality is that some investment will be required to transform an organization, analytical thinking does not necessarily cost anything.

Members who apply for loans online are willing to wait for an answer

This opinion was shared with me when I was onsite at a credit union observing underwriters make loan decisions in a centralized lending environment. As I was viewing the application queue, I noticed that some applications had been in queue for more than two days without receiving any sort of response. I inquired what the status of those applications might be. The response I received was that, since the credit union was understaffed, online applications were a lower priority than phone or branch applications, "because the member is sitting at home waiting." I suppose this might be true, but I can think of several arguments as to why it may not be true and industry data shows a shift in consumer expectations related to remote, online transactions[14]. But, the hypothesis can be easily tested.

---

[14] https://thefinancialbrand.com/70386/digital-lending-banking-ai-cx-trends/

A simple analysis of the different funding rates of applications by application source, such as phone, branch or online, could be employed. The credit union can also look at analyzing response times to applications to determine whether the decision turn-around time affects funding rates. You might also consider what is being required of the member to complete an online loan transaction. If, for example, the member ultimately must come to a branch to close a loan, then the potential of closing a loan may go down as borrowers choose more convenient options with other lenders despite most of the transaction being conducted online. As credit unions, we should not require loyalty of our members, but earn it. We earn it by taking the time to measure the effectiveness and efficiency of our product delivery process.

I can't trust credit scores

With any tool, a lack of understanding of its purpose effects our ability to use it effectively. I can't sink a screw with a hammer and I can't effectively hammer a nail with a screw driver, but both tools can be very effective. In lending risk seminars that I have conducted, I've asked lenders to define the purpose of a credit score. Out of several dozen lenders who were willing to raise their hands and answer the question, only a handful of them have ever had the correct answer. The credit score, no matter what model is used offers a current probability of default over the next 24 months. But, like all forecasts, the probability of default is subject to change based on the availability of more relevant information.

Take weather forecasts, for example. They are considered accurate up to 48 hours and are based on robust and complex models. But, they become significantly more accurate the closer you are to a weather event. My son, who is a trained meteorologist, can predict the probability of severe storms 48 hours away, but he can't accurately predict a tornado hitting your home until maybe five minutes before touch down. In the same way, if a member is going to default, the score is going to become more accurate in predicting that default the closer you observe the score relative to the actual default. In other words, borrower's credit scores change over time as the risk of default changes.

In the credit union, however, we often perform analysis of risk based on the forecast available at loan origination, which has little to do with the current risk of a loan based on current conditions. That would be like planning an outdoor picnic based on a weather forecast from seven days ago. Test my theory here and look at your current credit union reporting on the loan portfolio. If you are using 'risk-tier' in your reports, I guarantee the tier assignment is based on the origination credit score. It is no wonder then, that your results don't match what you might expect based solely on the origination credit score. Gathering new data and continually testing loan performance by current risk tranche is essential to accurately using a credit score in originating and pricing loans.

Chapter 4

The Big Data Hype

As you begin this chapter, I would like to caution you to not be discouraged, or offended, by its content. This chapter makes an attempt to define the data analytics landscape for credit unions as is stands at the end of 2018. The characterizations are generalized and do not apply to any specific technology vendor or credit union. It's likely that your credit union does not fit, exactly, into the characterization of all credit unions or, if you are a technology vendor, the examples provided may not apply to you. I am confident that the spirit of this chapter is spot on when it comes to the majority (greater than half), however.

Almost all innovative technology is introduced with a great deal of hype. Hype is the "extravagant or intensive publicity or promotion" of a product and serves a valuable purpose in marketing. Creating market buzz for new products, technologies and processes is essential to socializing innovative ideas in the marketplace, but hype can also confuse consumers of technology by overstating a products value or position. Throughout history, we have experienced hype and witnessed successes, failures, and products with a little bit of both. In this chapter we will look at some of the hype generated over data analytics in the credit union space and attempt to distinguish what is practical from what is impractical.

When television was originally introduced, it was panned as a fad or novelty and early programming was little more than radio content reformatted for the visual medium[15]. Of course, early television sets were expensive and even though they were introduced to the masses post World War II, few families were willing to invest in this emerging technology. For most, it was simply not that practical and it took a while for the television to "catch on". For example, the first TV broadcast license was issued in the U.S. in 1928, but by 1948 only 1 million U.S. homes, out of roughly 45 million, had television sets[16]. Color television technology was introduced in the early 1950's[17], but by 1972, twenty years later, only 50% of television sets were color. If you were alive in 1972, you and I both remember watching some programming that was still broadcast in black and white. These are very long adoption cycles in modern terms. It's for us to wonder if even the inventors, however, would have imaged how the television would transform modern society. One thing is sure, the tv set has certainly lived up to its hype, for good or bad.

---

[15] https://www.quora.com/Why-was-television-criticized-in-the-1950s

[16] http://www.datesandevents.org/events-timelines/08-television-invention-timeline.htm

[17] http://www.earlytelevision.org/color.html

In contrast to the television, the world has also witnessed products that have failed despite considerable hype. In 1985, the Coca-Cola company decided that their classic formulation, of what had become the world's favorite beverage, needed an overhaul[18]. Attempting to head off a fifteen-year decline in market share, and after considerable research and testing, Coca-Cola made the risky decision to change its premier cola formula to appeal to a greater number of consumers. For seventy-nine days in '85, American lives were up-ended, resulting in protests and hoarding of the remaining classic formulation stock. What is now believed to be history's biggest marketing blunder, New Coke received little to no adoption and the old formula was re-introduced in less than three months as Coca-Cola Classic. The event was so news-worthy that the ABC television network interrupted the broadcast of its most popular daytime drama, General Hospital, to announce Coca-Cola's decision to return its original formula to store shelves[19].

Ride-sharing, a more recent introduction to the consumer market, has promised to disrupt the transportation business, specifically taxi cabs and vehicle rentals. Promoters of products like Uber and Lyft have envisioned individuals abandoning the ownership of personal vehicles, no longer hailing taxi cabs from the street corner and/or bypassing the airport vehicle rental counter in lieu of summoning a ride from another private vehicle owner. There is no doubt that the technology used by companies like Uber and Lyft to hail rides has impacted the industry to some degree,

---

[18] https://www.coca-colacompany.com/stories/coke-lore-new-coke

[19] https://www.cbinsights.com/research/corporate-innovation-product-fails/

but the concept has not disrupted or displaced the existing taxi cab business[20]. I believe we can agree that the underlying technology of ride-sharing is not that different from the age-old taxi cab; you have a car, and you have a driver. The added technology, using mobile apps to summon a ride, has transformed the process of arranging for transportation, but can easily be adopted by more traditional providers moving forward. In other words, what makes Uber and Lyft's business model work can be easily adopted by market incumbents.

While the total impact of ride-sharing companies on the taxi cab industry is still being debated, what can be asserted is that the addition of services like Uber and Lyft have *expanded* the market[21]. Individuals who may have previously rented a vehicle or even chosen to drive their own vehicle in the past, are now choosing to use ride-sharing because it is more efficient than previously available choices and is perceived as preferable to hailing a cab. For example, college students use to designate a driver when going out to bar-hop. Today, they simply use Uber to take them from one club to another. It's much safer than the previous option and affords everyone the opportunity to participate in the revelry. It is likely, then, that the initial hype regarding total disruption will fall short, but after market adjustments the result will be that the ride sharing industry, as a whole, will be dramatically changed and expanded.

---

[20] https://www.forbes.com/sites/adigaskell/2017/01/26/study-explores-the-impact-of-uber-on-the-taxi-industry/

[21] http://blog.directpay.online/how-uber-revolutionized-taxi-industry

Data analytics, or Business Intelligence (BI), is not new and it would be a stretch to claim that it is disruptive. Decision support technology has existed for decades and BI disciplines are well established throughout many industries, such as education and healthcare. But, the use of data and BI in decision making for financial institutions is a relatively new thing, more so for credit unions than for banks. This is not a criticism but is more a recognition that credit union decision making has been based more on qualitative considerations than quantitative. However, we cannot ignore the disruptive potential of data-driven decision making on financial services in the future and we must find a balance between the individualized touch and decision efficiency and accuracy that benefits the member. New entrants in this space have taken a technology-first, data-driven, approach to offering new services and platforms for delivering consumer financial products. More so, regulatory requirements for financial institutions to demonstrate recognition and management of risk elevates data analytics to an existential imperative for both large and small credit unions alike (That sounded a little "Hypey" but hear me out.).

Nearly a decade ago, I began introducing data analytics to credit unions across the country. I felt a bit like an itinerant preacher moving from town to town preaching the gospel of Business Intelligence. Folks would look at me askew and challenge me with long-held credit union demagoguery (reminding me that that members are not numbers), but in some cases, they would welcome my message with hearty acceptance. The truth is, however, that encouraging the use of data analytics in decision making in credit unions was not exclusively my idea. It was the idea of regulators

69

that presented itself in the form of a risk letter published by the NCUA in 2005 related to Specialized Lending Activities and in 2010 related to Concentration Risk. More recently, credit unions have discovered the heavy data analytics requirement for calculating Current Expected Credit Losses, or CECL (pronounced See-Sill) as it is commonly known. The delayed enforcement of these requirements has allowed credit unions to push-back the implementation of data analytics and data-driven decision making, but the requirement has not been negated. Nonetheless, these requirements will not be going away, and you can be sure that regulators will point to these admonitions the next time we are in challenging economic times. Already, I have reports of examiners asking credit unions if they have recently tested their concentration risk policy.

In the first decade of the millennium, more credit unions began to expand product and service offerings to members, going well beyond typical deposit accounts and personal loans. One opportunity that arose from field of membership expansion, enabled by a change of federal in law in the latter nineties, was the ability for credit unions to participate in point-of-sale, or Indirect, auto lending. Credit unions began to acquire loans originated by auto dealers, sometimes from third-party aggregators, and these loans presented new inherent risks that did not exist in the typical direct member auto loan. While these new risks were real, regulators recognized that it was essential for credit unions to participate in this existing lending environment, but also recognized the importance for increased vigilance in relationship to risk management[22]. This concern

---

[22] https://www.ncua.gov/Resources/Documents/Risk/RSK2005-01.pdf

manifested itself in the form of Static Pool Analysis recommendations. This advisory suggested that lenders should analyze risk associated with specific pools of loans in isolation.

In 2010, subsequent to the economic meltdown of 2008 and 2009, regulators began to identify that financial institutions with high concentrations of particular loans, with similar characteristics impacted commonly by economic shifts, present an existential threat to credit unions. In this case, credit unions in some geographic areas found that their mortgage portfolios were severely under-collateralized as real estate values declined dramatically for probably the first time in modern history. We can readily recognize that similar concentrations in auto lending or commercial lending can have equally devastating effects on credit union loan performance under certain economic conditions. In response to these heightened risks, the NCUA published a letter to credit unions mandating that all credit unions establish Concentration Risk policies and put into place methods for measuring and monitoring risks throughout the credit union financial portfolio. Interestingly, beyond the mandate for a Concentration Risk Policy, this letter went a long way toward defining a data-driven decision culture for credit unions and prescribing the use of data warehouses and risk models while establishing the need for data governance from the credit union leadership down[23].

"Credit union management must emphasize the importance of maintaining comprehensive and accurate data for each risk area.

---

[23] https://www.ncua.gov/Resources/Documents/LCU2010-03Encl.pdf

This includes a quality control function to ensure that data entry and changes are accurate and timely.

The credit union should have a data processing system capable of warehousing data on various lines of business, commensurate with its size and complexity, to properly identify and measure concentration risk. For example, this would include maintaining information relevant to the loan portfolio such as loan type, interest rate, interest rate reset dates (if applicable), payment amount, payment shock (the potential increase in payment from an interest rate reset or conversion from interest-only to principal and interest payments), credit score (including original and updated periodically), collateral description, and collateral value (including original and updated periodically). Another example would include maintaining information relevant to the investment portfolio such as type, interest rate, collateral information, market value (original and updated periodically), and external rating (original and updated periodically). This is not an all-inclusive[sic] list, but rather a starting point for evaluating if the data processing system is capable of maintaining this type of data.

If the credit union does not have the data processing capability, management should contract with a third party to provide data warehousing and reporting. If management elects to pursue this route, examiners should review their initial and ongoing due diligence of the vendor to ensure it is in accordance with published guidance and safe and sound business practices."

-NCUA, March 2010

CECL presents a new challenge for all financial institutions. According to the American Bankers Association (ABA), the action of the Financial Accounting Standards Board (FASB) to change the way loan losses are accounted for by financial institutions is "the biggest change in bank accounting, ever."[24] While this is certainly true for the financial services industry, it is especially true for credit unions as, collectively, credit union data resources, essential for predictive modelling, are scarcer than those of their larger compatriots. This scenario has created an influx of data vendors into the credit union marketplace offering a plethora of seemingly similar, but strikingly different, solutions promising to quickly solve the data analytics problem for these financial institutions. This rush to the market and credit union's generally low familiarity with the regulation or the technology has provided the opportunity for increased hype for these solutions.

Keep in mind, stating that hype exists is not the same as suggesting that any individual hyped solution is not valuable. As stated above, hype is often necessary in the initial stages of technology introduction and adoption, but there are consequences for both the producer and consumer of technology if the solution cannot, or does not, deliver on the hype. One negative consequence is something that Gartner, a technology consulting group, refers to as the "trough of disillusionment". Gartner illustrates the Hype Cycle starting with a steep, upward curve at the introduction of

---

[24] http://www.arkbankers.org/ABA/Resource_Center/

73

technology followed by a sharp decline in enthusiasm, represented by a trough.   The Hype Cycle can be best illustrated by viewing the recent rise and fall of Bitcoin value from the end of 2016 to the end of 2018[25]. The Cycle, as defined by Gartner, is the result of a combination between high visibility over a brief period of time and the excitement of early adopters making significant investment in new technology, only to find that it doesn't fully deliver on its promise. As negative or cautious sentiment reverberates, and visibility begins to wane through the market, new-comers are hesitant to dive in and, instead, standby, watching to see how things develop. Considerable time and opportunity is often wasted while the market is stuck in this trough.

Currently, we are experiencing a high-level of hype in the credit union space regarding data analytics. This is not a criticism but simply an observation as hype can be good for socializing innovative ideas. We hear vendors and technology leaders talking about Big Data, Predictive Analytics, Prescriptive Analytics and Business Intelligence when many credit unions struggle to accurately define how to count your current members. Innovation and transformation are all the rage, but very little of that is actually happening in the real world. Terms such as Data Warehousing and Data Scientists are new to us but are being used more frequently and, in some cases, inaccurately creating confusion, which does the producers and consumers of technology no favors. It is a great fear of mine that credit unions will continue to delay the rapid adoption of data-

---

[25] https://www.cryptocurrencychart.com/chart/BTC/price/USD/linear/2015-12-27/2018-11-25

driven decision cultures or, worse yet, needlessly fall into the trough of disillusionment very quickly as they consider adopting these strategies.

While I have worked with a handful of credit union seeking to change their decision culture, to date, most communications that I have with credit unions about data analytics can be contributed to regulatory mandates, not an organizational data strategy. Examiners have specifically asked credit unions to test Concentration Risk policies, conduct Static Pool Analysis, or test their lending policies for disparate impact. These challenges are usually assigned to the credit union department most responsible for the problem in the first place and are not, typically, an organizational-level effort. A smaller, but growing, percentage of credit unions are talking about BI from a strategic position. Vendors have established conferences to gather data-minded people to ideate on data strategy and start-ups are entering the market with solution specific offerings. When I encounter many of these market participants, I like to ask them about client acquisition. I usually get a sheepish grin in response to my question, indicating that, while they are hopeful, they haven't become the next Jeff Bezos. Adoption of large scale data analytics within credit unions is still slow.

Very few credit unions, or providers, are discussing data analytics and business intelligence from an enterprise perspective, however, and trade organizations are doing little to foster conversations and innovations in data-driven decision making. There seems to be an assumption that this is a foregone conclusion. I have clients that are using, and paying for, two similar analytics products in the same credit union because individual department heads have directed the selection process to address their own department's needs. Disappointing, however, is how under-utilized many of these solutions are once implemented within the organization. In other words, credit unions are in a period of high visibility regarding data and there is high potential for entering a trough of disillusionment if proper education and planning does not occur to support enterprise transformation to data-driven decision cultures over the long-term.

In the spirit of education, I think it helpful to introduce some terms that you may encounter during your own transformation and properly define them here:

Data Scientist

The term Data Scientist is increasing in popularity, across all industry, as interest in data increases, however, the term is not synonymous with previously used terms applied to analytics, such as Data Analyst, for example. Unlike the term Flight Attendant which has become more appropriate than Steward or Stewardess, or Mail Carrier to replace Mailman, Data Scientist is not a new term to describe a previously defined role. According to Wikipedia, while the term data science has been used over the years, Harvard Business Review made Data Scientist a buzzword in 2012 when it named it the "sexiest job of the 21st century." I have seen the term best defined as an individual who understands the math/statistics, technology and business application of data. In credit union language, that would be someone who not only understands how to calculate key metrics but knows where to find the contributing data in the credit union's disparate business systems and how to transform analysis into information that credit union decision-makers can use to make decisions on products and services offered to members.

A database administrator or data architect can construct a database to store raw data but can't necessarily mine and integrate data in a way that is coherent to the end user. A data analyst may be able to create a report that informs you that your auto loan delinquency ratio is 120%. A business analyst can tell you that the data analyst's report is absurd but can't tell you how to correct it. But, a Data Scientist can do all these functions, streamlining the process and providing more accurate and timely results. A trained Data Scientist commands a higher salary relative to other people in the data value chain and it may not be a position for which many credit unions are currently budgeting. So, it's important that you get what you are paying for and you are budgeting for what you want to get.

Data Warehouse

When you first encounter this term, you might be tempted to infer that this simply identifies an exceptionally large database, and that is what we find in a lot cases when an organization says that they have a data warehouse. In reality, what they have is a really large, disorganized database, not a data warehouse. Most of us are familiar with the concept of databases as a storage facility for data. Our minds naturally think of a warehouse as lots of storage space. After all, your garage is a storage facility for your personal stuff and a warehouse is just a bigger place to store your stuff. But, you should consider the appropriate comparison to be more like your garage and an Amazon distribution center. As stated previously, both store stuff, but it is likely that you can find what you are looking for a lot faster, among millions of items, in an Amazon distribution center than you can in your own garage. In the same way, a true Data Warehouse is a specially designed database where data is stored and organized in a way to facilitate end user access that is timely and consistent. This involves the integration of data from multiple data sources, where raw data is stored in incongruent formats, into a single agreed upon format to be used by business users to make decisions.

Big Data

Big Data is often used to define the relative volume of data in the context of an organization. My Christmas card mailing list is small data and my prospective client list is big data, for example. However, Big Data most accurately refers to the total volume of existing data in the universe. Referencing Big Data infers that your organization is going beyond its walls to acquire data from external sources to integrate with internal data for decision making. For example, acquiring geolocation data from a member's mobile device and using that data to send tailored product offerings would be an example of using Big Data. Let's say your member has downloaded your credit union's mobile app and activated location services. If a debit card transaction originates from a vendor on the east side of town and your member's mobile device is located on the west side of town, you could generate an alert to the member and request a response to verify authorization for the transaction. If we are completely honest with ourselves, we can admit that we're not quite there yet as credit unions, but perhaps we have vendors who provide similar services. While

Big Data is interesting to talk about, it's probably hyperbole to suggest the primary use of Big Data is on our credit union's short-term roadmap.

"As A Service"

Several technology solutions are developed and sold "as a service". It has become a technology buzz-phrase. This basically means that the solution is sold as a subscription model and is typically cloud-based. In other words, you do not possess the software on premise and you often pay monthly license fees in perpetuity rather than a large, one-time price. Personally, I'm still waiting for someone to develop *Service as a Service* as a joke. Wouldn't that be funny? In fact, it may exist by now because technology developers are such funny people, but I've not seen it yet. While it is very popular to develop solutions as a service because it allows for lower costs, faster implementation and more robust features in many cases, there are questions to be asked when considering an "As a Service" solution. What makes "As a Service" affordable for smaller entities is that it is typically built for the masses and provides configurability over customization. In other words, the service can be highly flexible within the confines of available features, but you can forget about customizing the solution for your organization. Users are often forced to adopt the providers standardization rather than using their own process. For example, we know that credit unions refer to their customers as members. You may find that your analytics Software as a Service (SaaS) provider insists on the term customer. To integrate their system into your environment, you would be required to adopt that terminology. That is a basic example, but it illustrates how those constraints might have an impact on you and your organization.

****

I think the list above covers the big ones, but I may be compelled to revise this list in the future if the need arises.

The reason I took the initiative to define these terms is that a misunderstanding of them contributes to an existing chasm between most solution providers operating in the credit union space and the average credit union. To illustrate this, allow me to compare data as a river flowing through your operation, separating management from decisions. In order to use your data in decision making, you must be able to cross that river, but there currently is no bridge. On the decision side of the river, technology companies have begun building a bridge based on two primary assumptions. The first assumption is that they know what is best for the credit union, based on their experience or anecdotal information, and in the absence of specific requests from credit union clients. This is a practical assumption when you are trying to drive an innovative technology into a new market. The second assumption is that there is someone at the credit union prepared to initiate the building process from the management, or decision-maker, side. Very few vendors provide educational resources to help the decision-maker learn how to use data analytics. Often, there is no one on the credit union side with the requisite skill in data sciences or the empowerment to complete the bridge building project, so the two sides, from a decision-making standpoint, remain disconnected.

80

As result of the disconnect, credit unions, like many other companies by the way, may invest in data analytics technology that goes unused, or under-utilized, throughout the contract period. At the end of that period, the credit union may be disappointed with the results and stop the transformation process. This contributes to the disillusionment described above, in Gartner's Hype Cycle, and ultimately slows the transformation process to data-driven decision cultures. The smaller number of credit unions that do have the requisite resources to complete the bridge, in the meantime, are off to the races which, unfortunately, creates a competitive disadvantage between the 'haves' and the 'have-nots'.

Interestingly, James Dearsley, a self-described serial entrepreneur, suggests a way that can circumvent the trough of disillusionment that should be particularly compelling to credit unions. He suggests that collaboration can potentially soften a fall into disillusionment[26]. But, what does collaboration mean in the context of technology adoption and how can credit unions leverage its benefits? I think the first step in the process is to accept that, but for the largest of credit unions, it is highly unlikely that individual credit unions will invest in enterprise data science solutions. The second step would be for current technology vendors, in the credit union space, to provide better access to data and allow for analytics platforms to integrate more readily. This takes the burden off the credit union to employ resources for extracting and transferring data from one system to another. But, the issue is that many software providers attempt to build proprietary analytics features into their software and resist

---

[26] http://www.jamesdearsley.co.uk/proptech-hype-cycle/

making operational system data available to other providers. The third recommendation I would offer would be that current analytics product vendors collaborate among themselves to consolidate their existing single solution products into a more robust, integrated solution platform. I believe my friends at OnApproach, a Minnesota-based CUSO, have started this process by creating the central component to a data analytics platform, the Data Warehouse, and providing applications through third parties that directly connect to this data, but this only takes care of the technology component. Remember, Data Science also requires mathematics/statistics and domain expertise. Vendors like OnApproach must also collaborate with domain experts to increase adoption and engagement with their technology.

It was my goal, when I launched CUBI.Pro, a business intelligence consulting firm, to eventually create a Credit Union Service Organization (CUSO) with the specific purpose of providing data science services to credit unions and offer assistance in selecting the right technology for their specific implementation. In fact, it is my argument that sharing data science resources among credit unions is exactly what the CUSO model is designed for. Throughout credit union history, credit unions have joined together to create solutions that help all credit unions level the playing field in financial services. CO-OP Financial Services allows credit unions to broaden their presence via shared-branching, outsourced member services, and an ATM network. CU Direct has provided a credit union owned platform for credit unions to use to originate Indirect vehicle loans and engage in point of sale lending. Certainly, there are many more successful examples of this type of collaboration. A business intelligence CUSO would provide credit unions, of all sizes, the opportunity to leverage shared data science resources, technology, and larger, shared data sets.

One of the greatest challenges for credit unions seeking a data-driven decision culture, and the technology vendors trying to assist them, is limited access to the credit unions' own data. Many legacy platforms do not collect enough relevant data to be used in decision making, ancillary systems such as Loan Origination Systems (LOS), or servicing platforms, make it difficult to extract data and third-party servicing companies provide credit unions with little more than basic reporting on account management. If you step back and consider all the possible data points that can be collected about any member and/or transaction, you quickly realize that the core data processing system doesn't have the available fields for storing the data and for performance reasons, historic data is quickly archived, leaving the credit union with little historic perspective. Many of these same system providers make it difficult and costly to integrate third-party software, presumably to protect their own product sales, which restricts many credit union's ability to transfer data from one system to the other. Simply put, the process for collecting and accessing data in the typical credit union just isn't that easy.

Current data and analytics technology vendors are each trying to attain profitability by providing narrowly focused products that purport to solve single data analytics problems for credit unions. Rarely do these vendors join forces to leverage their shared knowledge and expertise to extend their product capabilities. As a result, to be honest, few have been able to profit from providing data and analytics products to credit unions specifically and, if they have, those profits are tentative at best. The reason for this is that the data culture in the credit union space is still developing and many solutions are yet to be proven. This is not to infer that all vendors struggle for profitability or that the future is without hope. But, too often these solutions are over-built and too complex, hoping to meet everyone's possible need. Whenever a software provider tries to provide everything to all people, they often miss the quality mark in the features they do provide. Consolidation, simplification, and collaboration are three ways vendors could gain early and sustained traction in the credit union space.

This may sound like doom and gloom to you, but that is not my intent. What I am attempting to do is accurately define the current state of data analytics in the credit union space and help you discern between the hype and reality. The truth is, very few credit unions have reached a point of consistently making data actionable, so if you are struggling today or are considering starting your data journey soon, you should know that you are not that far behind. But, the proper response is not to stand on the sideline and wait. You will quickly find yourself behind the curve. Instead, use what you have learned to make educated decisions about your credit union's next steps.

Chapter 5

Common Transformation Roadblocks and Hurdles

It's my hope that the previous chapter on hype hasn't killed your enthusiasm for a transformation to a data-driven decision culture, as it really is essential for any business in the digital age. This dose of reality should help provide some sobriety, however, and level expectations. The transformation to a data-driven decision culture is a change that takes some time. The amount of time required depends on the commitment of credit union leadership to finish and an avoidance of some of the key hurdles and roadblocks that organizations encounter as they attempt a change from intuitive decision making to data-driven decisions.

Existing Culture

One inherent roadblock to culture change, of any kind, is the existing culture. Old habits are hard to break and require new learning. I'm reminded of my own habit change, just a few years ago. Some people find it hard to believe that I was once a cigarette smoker. I must admit, I actually enjoyed smoking for a number of years. I was such a committed smoker that when my wife left the house with my car keys one day, I convinced myself to run a mile to the seven-eleven to get a fresh pack, when I found I had ran out. As I left the store with my full pack of smokes, no doubt panting heavily, it hit me that, if I could run a mile for a pack of cigarettes, I could run a mile to save my life. I soon dropped the smoking habit and began running instead. I lost forty pounds over about six months and won a first-place medal in my first 5K run about a year later. At my 50-year-old physical, I received a clean bill of health, except for an ulcer which is a whole other story. Apparently, I have another lifestyle change to undergo.

So, why did I decide to make a radical change in my life? When I was seventeen years old, my dad had his first of four heart attacks; he was 41 years old. He is still alive today, but only after a major bypass surgery and a couple of additional procedures along the way. Before the time I was 40 years old, three of my wife and I's four parents and all our grandparents had all passed away from various diseases. Besides my dad, my wife and I are now the oldest people in our family! None of the family members who died smoked cigarettes or drank alcohol. Every time I would visit the doctor, she would tell me the same thing; you are healthy now, but if you keep doing what you are doing, you will die young. It took several reruns of that conversation for it to resonate with me and I determined that I didn't want to die before I had reached my full potential. I finally took the initiative to make the change I knew was required.

Since the mid-1990s, credit union regulators have been recommending that credit unions use data to inform decisions about risk and opportunity. In a recent survey conducted by Best Consulting and OnApproach, one-third of credit unions responded that they do not believe data is important to their business strategy, while another third have a strategy for integrating data into decision making[27]. The rest of credit unions are somewhere in the middle. I'm not sure that the credit unions who "say" they don't value data mean it, just like when I used to say I "enjoyed smoking". I think these credit unions understand the reality, but if I were to guess, they are not interested in taking part in the transformation process that is required when one views data to be valuable in decision-making. More than likely, these credit union leaders will need to be able to visualize the future and determine, like I did that day outside seven-eleven, the result of transformation is better than the future prospect of the current state. In reality, I believe these credit unions who are not using data in decision making are actually reluctant to start a transformation without some form of guaranteed return on investment.

---

[27] http://blog.onapproach.com/newsroom/mixed-results-for-future-of-data-analytics-in-credit-unions-2018-mid-year-credit-union-data-analytics-survey-reveals-surprising-trends

HiPPO Decision Process

An intuitive decision culture is often plagued with the HiPPO decision process. HiPPO stands for the Highest Paid Persons Opinion. It makes sense that the person in charge, who is often the highest paid person, prefers to make decisions about business strategy. Therefore, we have leaders and followers. However, this creates a problem if the person in charge bases their decisions solely on their experience and intuition. It is difficult to innovate when you only consider what you know. Organizations that rely heavily on intuition and opinion, very rarely create a competitive advantage. In order to succeed in transforming your credit union from intuitive decision making to data-driven decision making, it is incumbent upon leaders in the organization to insist on using data.

Cognitive Bias

Another issue that plagues a culture shift to data-driven decisions is Cognitive Biases. Cognitive Biases, as described in Chapter 3, are the inherent thinking processes that we have as humans that plague our intuitive approach to decision making. In an intuitive decision culture, we are convinced that we can make better decisions on our own, rather than those based on supporting data, especially within our domain of experience. It is difficult, for example, to convince lenders that longer-term loans perform better than shorter-term loans, at least when comparing sixty-month terms and seventy-two-month terms. There is actually a cultural bias against long-term borrowing for automobiles that impacts our decision making. Our cognitive bias forces us to rely on experience and fall for the fallacy, supported by public opinion, that the longer a loan is, the riskier it could be. However, I have analyzed several loan portfolios and found, often, the opposite is true. So, we charge 50 basis points more for 72-month loans than we do 60-month loans and argue, if nothing else, there is a risk that rates will rise over the longer term. Interestingly, however, the difference between a 5-year ARM and a 7-year ARM is less than 20 basis points at many credit unions. Therefore, lenders are still influenced by a bias towards shorter-term *auto* loans, regardless of interest rate risks, because interest rate risk is not reflected in mortgage loans to the same degree as it is in auto loans, even though the risk is the same. Cognitive Bias impacts intuitive decision-making to a higher degree than we even imagine.

Data Quality

Many organizations, and especially credit unions, find that accessing good data for analysis poses a significant hurdle to transformation to data-driven decisions. After all, without data it is extremely difficult to be data-driven. The fact of the matter is, credit unions are not without data. To the contrary, credit unions have lots of data, but it is often difficult to access and, when it is accessible, it is often not in a state ready for analytics. This single factor, while not the sole reason, is why credit union leaders postpone a transformation to data-driven decision making. I refer to it as the 'blind curve', because as we initiate the process of transformation, it is not too far in the journey when we come to the realization that data acquisition is much more difficult than we even imagined.

There are no easy shortcuts to issues with data, but these issues never get resolved if they are never addressed and the good news is that there are a lot of resources available to credit unions today that did not exist ten years ago. There are organizations that offer consulting, like my own CUBI.Pro, with a specific slant toward credit unions. These organizations have worked with many credit unions and technology vendors, so they can apply some skills to shortening the data integration process. OnApproach, a CUSO based in Minnesota, is providing credit unions with data warehousing facilities that are relatively inexpensive and are reasonably easy to deploy. Then there are products like Visible Equity, Lending Insights and BankBI that provide cloud-based data warehousing and formatted reporting with dashboarding capabilities. No matter which you choose, there are some common data issues that will plague every analytics project.

The first data issue that typically arises is that the data required for analysis simply wasn't collected, or if it was collected, it was not stored in electronic format. This reminds me of the way we used to store credit application data years ago, before PC's could be found on every desktop. Back in the day, we used to have to refer to the 'loan file' which was a manila file folder stored in a filing cabinet. You use to have to go to the file room and request the loan file. The clerk would go back to the file cabinets and pull the file you requested and hand it over to you. Then, you had to make copies of the pertinent documents in the file, like a credit application, and return the file folder back to the file clerk. This, of course, made large-scale data analytics impossible.

Today, even with modern technology, data is still not collected or stored for several reasons. One reason it may not be stored is that it is considered irrelevant. If you are a credit union that uses a generic loan or member application, it is likely that you do not use all the information collected on these forms. So, the irrelevant data is dismissed. Another reason data is not collected is because those who collect it perceive that there is no place to store it. Core data processing systems only have room for so many data fields; so, when there are no more fields for data, we stop collecting data. And finally, data is not collected because it is not mandated to be collected. As folks fill in forms, if the field isn't required, it is 'tabbed' through with the belief that, if its required later, it can be filled in. Therefore, if the information is never requested then it doesn't get stored and it doesn't exist for data analytics. Take the 'number of dependents' field on a credit application, for example. That information may not be used to decide on a loan application, but later the credit union may want to analyze the performance of loans based on the number of dependents supported by the borrower.

Discretionary field inputs can also create 'bad' data. Take it from someone who has managed a software product, deciding when and how to enforce field integrity is a challenging endeavor. As soon as you decide to make an email field mandatory, for example, you come across an instance where you absolutely cannot collect an email address and the process fails. Some research has found that requiring information encourages people to provide false information when they are unable to provide the information requested. For example, if your form requires an email address and I don't want to provide my real one, I might enter 'mickey.mouse@disney.com'. But, you still want to collect every possible, accurate email address for applicants that you can so that you can use it later for engagement purposes. So then, you have to find a balance between requiring fields to be completed and encouraging those entering data to provide as much accurate information as possible when fields are not required.

Allowing free form entries into fields probably causes the most issues as data entered is subject to users' preferences and ability to spell words correctly. Take something as simple as a state abbreviation. It is likely users know how to abbreviate their own state name, but what if it's a state they seldom ever come across? Will they know the correct abbreviation? My experience says that they won't. I once sat observing a lending department employee boarding loans on a credit union's core system. As he entered the vehicle description for a loan, I asked this question, "who decides what abbreviation you use for Chevrolet?" He said, "I do." It was clear to me that this practice was prone to creating bad data. If there are no consistent rules as to how free-form data is entered into the data base, you are almost certain to get as many variations as there are people entering data. One friend of mine at a credit union in Portland, OR once told me that she didn't know how many ways there were to spell, or misspell, Portland until she became a data analyst and began working with her credit union's data.

Changing data from what was originally input into a database causes an entirely different problem and considerable angst. I'm not just referring to correcting incorrect data, but I'm primary talking about the practice of overwriting data because it is perceived to not be relevant any longer. There are two examples of this that pop-up nearly 100% of the time in credit union datasets. The first example is the loan type of a loan, such as auto, motorcycle, personal, etc. When loans are charged off, many credit unions change the loan type to signify the loan is charged off, like 'L99' for example. It becomes extremely difficult to analyze loan performance by loan type, in the future, when this type of origination data is changed. Another example I have seen is when new borrower credit scores are acquired; the previous score is overwritten with a new score. Obviously, a borrower's credit score from two years ago is irrelevant to a current credit decision but tracking borrowers' credit scores over time is important to predicting borrower behavior in the future and how those changes may affect borrower risk. For example, a borrower with a 720 score today but a 640 score a year ago is much different than a borrower with a 720 score today who had a 790 score a year ago. One borrower's risk rating is improving while the others is deteriorating, yet they have the same score.

Archived data is almost as worthless as data that was never collected in the first place. Granted, archiving data is essential for disaster recovery but, if we are honest, we will admit that we hope that never happens. Archived data is of very little use for analytics. The trouble is, it is especially difficult to conduct trending analysis if only a few months history is currently available, and the remainder of the historic data has been archived. No one is much interested in reloading archived data for a single analysis to be completed. What is especially frustrating is when a credit union does decide to do what it takes to restore some of this archived data, I.T. resources are often scarce, making the process take weeks or months. By the time the data is available, the need for the data has already passed.

Finally, when it comes to data, stale data can be frustrating as well. You may be thinking, at this point, didn't he just tell us not to overwrite old data? Well, yes, I did just say that. But, I didn't intend to suggest that new, up-to-date data shouldn't be acquired. Just don't overwrite the old data. There are several data points that could and should be updated over time, such as collateral values, credit scores as mentioned above, and income for account owners. You may want to collect the IP address data for members using your online banking system. Continually saving this information as it is produced provides the financial institution with robust member behavior information. All this data can be used for future analysis.

Scarce Resources

In addition to the challenges that data presents for the organization attempting to transform itself to a data-driven decision culture, scarce resources can present equal, if not greater, challenges. One mistake that organizations make when beginning a transformation journey is attempting to make the transition without making any changes to its current human resources allocation. A complete transformation may require re-allocated, additional, and/or improved resources. What often happens in credit unions when they begin their data journey is they start the process by purchasing analytics software or data storage technology from an outside vendor. Immediately, the I.T. team is assigned the task of working with the vendor to extract data from existing systems. This strategy would make complete sense if the I.T. department didn't have other, competing priorities. The primary purpose of I.T. departments in most organizations is to keep the business systems up and running and secure. This means that if the data processing system is offline, then I.T. must get it back online as soon as possible. If the email system is not working, they must get it back up and running again, immediately. These issues existed before any data initiatives and the credit union was perfectly resourced for these occurrences. In other words, while a fully transformed organization may find efficiencies when data is engaged in the operation, those efficiencies do not exist in the initial stages and a data project requires a great deal of attention to complete. If dedicated resources are not assigned, the project will lag due to interruptions by common, everyday events. Some organizations find it helpful to outsource these tasks to provide available resources as needed.

Another resource that is critical to the transformation process is someone who plays the role of project manager or a project management team. This can be a data governance team, a Data Scientist, or maybe even an outside consultant. A common misconception is that the transformation to a data-driven decision-making culture is simply about data access, but there is much more to it than that. A complete inventory of data sources is required. Requirements need to be gathered from key stakeholders. Definitions for measurements and dimensional data need to be agreed upon. And, the proper technologies need to be chosen. Some entity, whether it is a team or individual, needs to lead all the activities associated with the transformation and while there is a temptation to assign this to existing I.T. resources, these activities are better led by someone, or some group, which understands how data will be used in making business decisions.

Data Literacy

Data Literacy is another issue faced when organizations attempt to transform to a data-driven decision culture. Data literacy is defined by TechTarget as the "ability to derive meaningful information from data"[28], but I think this definition even falls short and I prefer the following definition provided by Purdue University, which describes data literacy as the ability to "use, understand and manage data[29]" for business decisions. For example, you may have seen a marketing executive argue that direct mail campaigns are ineffective because the return on investment is too low. On the surface, this argument makes sense. Yes, if the return does not exceed the cost and effort put into the campaign, it makes sense that the campaign is not effective. So, there you have it, meaningful information from data. Some decisions seem to be so obvious that they don't require any real data analytics. The same would be true for high charge-offs in the recreational vehicle portfolio. If it hurts, stop doing it. The two examples above are not really examples of data literacy, even though they meet the standard of the previous definition.

---

[28] https://whatis.techtarget.com/definition/data-literacy

[29] https://www.slideshare.net/Library_Connect/slides-research-data-literacy-and-the-library-70689154

Let's look at the first example. The hypothesis is that direct mail campaigns are not effective. The data used to not reject, or confirm, the hypothesis is that the return for the effort and cost is not enough to make it worth the while. Couldn't it also be true that the offer made in the direct mail campaign did not appeal to the recipients and the low response rate had nothing to do with the offer delivery method? A person who is data literate would understand how to properly test the hypothesis to determine what is fact and what is fiction. To properly determine whether a marketing method was effective or not would be to run several controlled tests, sending different offers to separate groups or repeating offers at different rates for different groups to determine whether response is affected by the offer, the number of times the offer is repeated or, in fact, the delivery method. Just because a decision refers to data, as in the initial example, does not mean that it is data-driven.

Common sense alone should clue you into whether the confirmation of a hypothesis has been arrived at correctly, or not. I like to use what I call the swimming pool test. When I was in kindergarten, I was at the pool in the apartment complex where we lived, just outside Randolph AFB, with my dad and my older brother. My dad and brother were in the pool splashing around and I was at the edge of the pool, afraid to jump in. I didn't know how to swim, and I was afraid I would drown. My dad was trying to coax me in, but I was resistant. I still remember something my dad said to me that eventually convinced me to jump. He asked me, "Do you see all of these people in the pool having a good time? No one is drowning. What makes you think you will drown?" That did it; I jumped and as this writing will attest, I did not drown. When you step out and make a statement, like the one above, that direct mail campaigns do not work, it might be a good idea to, first, take a look to see if others are doing it effectively. If direct mail campaigns don't work, why are there so many mailings in your mailbox every day? If decisions seem to conflict with what your common sense says, you may want to dig deeper than a superficial assessment. This requires proper testing and analysis.

Data literacy requires that you go beyond a superficial assessment of data. You need to be able to explain 'why' something works or doesn't work. Look at the second example from above regarding RV loans. It is highly likely that even with a high number of charge-offs, there were a considerable number of RV loans that performed well. Many lenders have decided to 'throw the baby out with the bathwater' based on just a little bit of data. A data literate team would dig deeper. They would segment the RV portfolio by credit grade, loan-to-value ratio, income, age of borrower, type of collateral and other loan and borrower attributes to determine if there is a significant difference in the performance of one segment and another. My hint to you, based on the experience of observing dozens of credit union portfolios, is that there will be shared characteristics of those loans that charged-off that can be mitigated in future underwriting. Proper testing and evaluation will prevent your credit union from decisions that negatively impact your potential for growth in the future.

Internal Conflict

Internal conflict over sharing of data creates walls that are difficult to scale to create a more collaborative data-driven decision environment.

When individual departments have been responsible for collecting data, self-reporting on performance and conducting their own analytics, there is a reluctance to share data with other departments in the organization. I remember when I first began offering loan portfolio management software to credit union lenders, I was shocked by how many prospects were not that interested in the product. The product performed well, provided amazing statistics, and helped lenders gain insight into portfolio performance that was not easily obtained through typical spreadsheets and reports. While no one ever said this to me, outright, I suspect that some of those lenders were not comfortable with the level of transparency the software provided. Despite the frustration we have all experienced in meetings where we argue about the validity of one person's data over another's, we may not be quite ready to surrender that fight to an unbiased "third-party", even if that third-party is a software solution.

Perceived Costs

It's often believed that the cost to transform to a data-driven decision culture cannot be justified in smaller financial institutions. While it is true that building an infrastructure to facilitate the storage and free flow of data in your organization can be expensive, incremental changes, progressing ever-closer to the ideal over time, can be accomplished on a budget. Currently available technologies allow even small organizations to analyze data that couldn't have previously been analyzed on a budget. Having said that, calculating the cost and benefits must include not only gains in production but also opportunities to cut the costs of operations. For example, if your average auto loan charge-off is $5,000 and you can prevent two charge-offs per year by conducting a default analysis of your loan portfolio, that would provide you with enough money to purchase most of the commonly used analytics software available on the market today. However, if building a data warehouse to conduct this simple analysis would cost you over $100 thousand, it would be cost prohibitive. It is important to understand the scale of your data projects to properly determine the investment that needs to be made. Most credit unions, for example, do not require a data warehouse to generate meaningful data analysis, at least not at the outset. It is my fear that many credit unions are under the impression that a data warehouse is required.

Everything is Fine

Finally, when things are going well in the organization, it is difficult to find a reason to change, even if your decision-making process is archaic. But, even this position is based on fallacy. Just because things are going well, doesn't mean they are going as well as they could be. Because your financial institution is profitable doesn't mean you are growing at the same pace as your market, gaining market share, or even serving your current members as well as you could. Further, when the health of the organization changes, it will be difficult to determine what needs to be adjusted to improve performance as there are no historic measurements. If an organization cannot identify what they are doing well with solid analytics, it will be hard to tell what the organization is not doing well when things go the other direction.

Chapter 6

Creating an Enterprise Data-Driven Culture Transformation Strategy

Much has been written about strategy. I will not try and outdo the great strategist of the past by attempting to redefine strategy or suggest that an Enterprise Data-Driven Culture Transformation (EDDCT) Strategy is any different than any other strategy at its core. But I think it is helpful to look at what a well-defined EDDCT strategy should consist of and how your organization will benefit from having one, if it is seeking to incorporate data into decision-making. A survey of credit unions, conducted in 2018 by BIG Solutions and OnApproach[30], found that nearly half of credit unions said that they have a data strategy in place. Yet, anecdotally, the dozens, if not hundreds, of credit unions I have worked with over the last several years have had a high degree of difficulty providing the minimum amount of data required for analysis. Either I have not had the opportunity to engage these credit unions with a strategy in place, or the sample of

---

[30] https://www.cutimes.com/2018/11/16/many-credit-unions-with-no-clear-data-analytics-st/

credit unions surveyed above were not representative of the whole. It is not a criticism to point out the data challenges of credit unions, it's simply an honest assessment of the current state. But, credit unions are not unlike many other small businesses in this regard. That said, an organization must decide if the status quo is acceptable. If not, the first step is to develop a strategy for transformation.

I recently worked with a credit union to develop a transformation strategy to create a data-driven decision culture. The project got off to a rough start as expectations were mis-aligned, to some degree, as they are with many strategic planning sessions. As it turns out, the credit union leadership was looking for a transformation roadmap, not a strategy. In other words, they were tempted to skip the strategy stage and immediately define action steps. Do this, then do that. One executive commented after reviewing the initial draft, "This doesn't tell us anything we don't already know."

My reply to that comment was, "Well then, why did no one bother to write it down?"

Thankfully, all my engagements do not start off quite so rough, but it doesn't surprise me when it comes to strategy engagements. The truth is, no one likes to work on strategy. I have lead strategy development and I have participated in strategy development. It's really not a lot of fun. If you ask a football running back how to win a football game, they are going to say you win by scoring points. If you ask a football coach the same question, he is going to talk about defense, offense, statistics, and game planning. Creating strategy is simply not as fun and exciting as execution. So, it's no surprise that team members want to skip the strategy development altogether and move right into execution.

I should probably back up a bit and explain how it is I thought I could get away with submitting a strategy for review that provided an organization's leadership with nothing new. My first response to that inquiry is that the characterization was not entirely true. I would follow that up with an acknowledgement that there are probably individuals in any organization who have a lot of the knowledge that would end up in a strategy document but, if this knowledge is siloed or not disseminated throughout the organization, it does not constitute and enterprise strategy. A big part of strategy development is mining information from various internal sources and integrating ideas into a unified document. Any plan relying on individuals to step up and do their job at the right time is not an effective way of leading an organization to success. While you may have the expectation that your lending manager will provide insightful information about portfolio performance, she may not. You may assume that your CMO is properly assessing ROI on every marketing campaign, but he may not be. The point it is, while talent is critical, it must be guided to be effective.

My son, Andrew, is a captain in the U.S. Air Force. Strategy is a very military word and military leaders spend a lot of time on training and strategy. If Andrew is not flying, he is planning or training. Why do they spend so much time training and planning? The answer is in the results. For all the time spent strategizing, the result is usually flawless execution. Andrew is a Weapons Systems Officer, or 'Wizzo', on the B-1 Bomber, affectionately known as "The BONE". Having had the opportunity to view this weapon up close, the BONE is an awesome aircraft with amazing capabilities. It falls under the classification of 'strategic' bomber. The technology that makes the systems on that plane work together is very complex and it takes a great deal of time to learn. Think about this, the military is so confident in its training and planning capabilities that it puts multi-million-dollar weapons in the hands of young men and women who are still paying the highest automobile insurance rates.

My son graduated with a Bachelor of Science degree in Meteorology from Texas A&M University. He then spent several weeks in Officer Training School (OTS) in Montgomery, AL and then, upon graduation from OTS, spent another several months learning to be an Air Force aviator. After intense training to be an aviator, he spent several more months learning specifically how to do his job on the B-1. He was more than a couple years into his Air Force career before he flew his first combat mission. Even still, one of the things that amazes me, even more than the training and learning required, is how much time he and his cohorts spend planning missions every day. In other words, the execution phase, or flying a mission, is extremely brief in comparison to the time spent training for and planning the mission. It might be more appropriate to refer to these men and women as strategist rather than aviators based solely on the allocation of their work.

Why does our military spend so much time on training and planning? I like to think it is because they take their mission very seriously. What is their mission? Protecting the freedom of U.S. citizens and like-minded allies around the world. For one-hundred years, the U.S. military has been called upon to settle the world's conflicts and, with few exceptions, they have succeeded in doing so. Everyone must show up and do the job they were trained to do, and their leaders have the responsibility to ensure they are properly equipped and prepared. As a child, when my dad was in the service, I remember there was no such thing as a real holiday and I recall there was rarely a vacation that wasn't somehow impacted by my dad's work. What's my point? Quite simply, our willingness to train and plan is an indicator of how committed we are to our organization's mission. No doubt, commitment to a defined outcome requires commitment to a plan.

It is possible that your organization is not committed to a transformation to a data-driven decision culture. If that is the case, then I presume you are reading this book purely for entertainment. It is perfectly okay if your desire is to continue to rely on intuitive decision making; it's still a free country thanks to the men and women referenced above. However, you need to know that as the next decade unfolds, your organization will struggle to find a competitive advantage and growth will be unattainable without the use of data in decision-making. If you do think that data-driven decision making is the way of the future, then developing an organizational strategy for transformation will be the key.

Where to Start?

Every journey has an origin. Except people like my dear wife, Angie, most people don't just wander around aimlessly and then claim they have reached their destination at some arbitrary point. In the same way, once you've made the decision to begin your data journey, it will be important to define, as an organization, what the destination of that journey will be. It's not as simple as saying, "we want to use data to make decisions." If a climber decides they are going to climb Mt. Everest, they don't just say, "I'm going to climb a mountain." No, instead, they say, "I'm going to climb Mt. Everest!" The former statement hedges the bet a little. The latter says something big and specific. Climbing any mountain is quite a fallback position from climbing the highest mountain on Earth. There is a small mountain range in south-central Oklahoma called the Arbuckle Mountains that fits the more general destination defined above, just in case. But, no one can argue that it would be the same as the experience of those who have touched the peak of the mountain that touches the heavens.

Defining your data destination may be a difficult first step as it relies upon making a statement about a future state without really knowing how you might get there. That's what makes the journey so much fun. Understand, however, that no matter how lofty your goal may be, it is quite probable that it will not exceed the data goals of a Google, Netflix, or Amazon. Not that you desire your organization become like any of these, the important thing to understand is that, no matter how lofty your target destination may be, some organization in the world has probably been able to achieve it. In other words, we know that it is possible given the right planning, preparation and resources. The only question is whether your organization is committed to getting there. If not, you may want to shoot for a more attainable destination.

For demonstration, allow me to throw out a proposed destination. Not that I would argue that this should be the same destination for every organization, but for demonstration purposes, it will be helpful as we proceed through the steps of creating a strategy to reference an example. Let's say that our organization's data destination is, "The XYZ Credit Union will be committed to making every critical business decision impacting our internal and external clients using a data-first mentality, using data to inform our direction and validate our decisions." Now, let's peel this destination apart and see how it works.

What does it mean to be committed to making every *critical* business decision impacting internal and external clients using a data-first mentality? It's likely that you are not necessarily going to do a complete data analysis on paint colors for your office space as it is most likely not critical to your business. It's a matter of taste or preference. But, you will use data to inform a decision about the location of your business as it will impact both internal and external clients. The location of a business is not, or should not be, a matter of taste or preference. Therefore, making data-driven decisions should not paralyze your business by consuming it into the vortex of analysis paralysis for every decision. One should be able to classify mission critical and non-critical decisions.

This destination goal also states that data will 'inform' our direction. This is very important as business leaders often determine a direction intuitively and then use data to make decisions related to how to implement that decision. When a competitor moves on a product offering, we intuitively want to follow them in order to remain competitive. Only then, after making the initial investment, we find that there is no profit to be made. This is wasteful and time-consuming. On the other hand, we should use data that provides direction for decision making and base our decisions on where the data points our organization, even if it doesn't point us in the same direction as our competitors. Instead of following competitors, we should lead them or perhaps decide to let them follow their own folly. This is only an example, so I don't need to spend much time convincing you of its practicality. I just wanted to point out a few things that make this a higher-level destination that simple using data to make decisions.

I'm reminded, at this point, of a project that I worked on in a credit union where I worked in the early 2000's. I was responsible for launching an indirect lending program in the city of Dallas, TX. Prior to me coming aboard, the credit union had decided to use the CU Direct CUDL platform to support its indirect lending. Again, this was back in the early 2000's when CU Direct wasn't well known in the market and there were two well-known competing platforms, DealerTrack and Route One, that had an established market presence. Furthermore, the other credit unions that were participating in indirect lending around Dallas had chosen to use third-party origination programs instead of managing the entire process internally, as we had done. In other words, our credit union had decided to take a different path than our closest, like-sized competitors.

Three months into our program, my credit union's CEO became agitated that other credit unions around us were reporting tremendous growth and success in the market while we struggled to achieve any traction at all. Our biggest issue, at the time, was that we had chosen a technology partner, CU Direct, that was not "Plug & Play" in the market and the programs chosen by other credit unions were using already established platforms. This meant that we not only had to convince an auto dealer to do business with the credit union, we also had to convince them to do business with CU Direct.

The CEO of my credit union dispatched me to talk to the third-party providers that the other credit unions had chosen to see if we had an opportunity to recover our program by choosing a different path. I did as he asked, gathered the data, and ultimately made a recommendation. What I discovered by conducting the analysis was that the other programs did not support long-term success, but more of a grab-and-go strategy over which the credit unions had little control. The recommendation I made to the CEO, at significant risk to my status of employment, was that, if our desire was to create a sustainable program, we should double down on our current choice and work diligently to gain market share instead of making a switch. Just over one year later, most of the other credit unions had exited the marketplace either because their portfolios were not performing well or because they had run out of money to lend. The third-party providers eventually left the market and, in fact, do not exist today. Sometimes, I just get lucky.

Initially, your destination may not be as lofty as the proposed destination I have provided, but it still requires some specificity. We could, instead, say that we want to experiment with enterprise data to determine the best use of data in decision making. This is certainly an intermediate goal but is specific as to what the organization wants to accomplish. It also informs us as to where we want to stop on this journey, preventing scope-creep. In this case, we want to stop short of actually using data in business decisions. Instead, we want to focus our efforts on experimentation. If this were our stated destination, being specific would prevent us from losing focus on experimentation, which can be quite valuable. The problem is, few organizations have the resources to commit to experimentation without eventually bringing that learning into the operation of the business. Either way, below I provide some critical elements that should play a role in your EDDCT strategy.

Interview Stakeholders

What is a stakeholder? A stakeholder is defined as an individual with an interest or concern in something. Who these individuals are will be different depending upon the organization and the destination of your journey. Using our originally defined destination above, I think we have three distinct categories of stakeholders, decision-makers, internal clients, and external clients. Obviously, these categories may overlap, but this definition could represent a lot of people. One could even say that it is everyone impacted by your organization. It may not be necessary to interview every one of them, but it is important to interview a representative sample. Some organizations are tempted to leave voices out of the discussion under the auspices of time-savings, but this may actually be a short-cut designed to focus on the things that leadership thinks are important. This will surely result in missed opportunities. It is important to take this step of the process seriously because this is where new information is gained, and future challenges are identified.

Decision-Makers

I would interview *every* internal business decision-maker. These are the people who are empowered to make decisions regarding how the organization employs its resources to produce revenue. I make this distinction as there are people who make decisions affecting your business that business decision-makers are not involved with daily. There are buying decisions made by consumers and cultural decisions made by employees that are not necessarily related to investments, product delivery, and/or operations. Business decision-makers require a very specific set of business data for decision-making and the decisions they make, often, have the highest impact on business profitability. Here are some questions that help define business leaders' data requirements that you may want to ask in a stakeholder interview.

How do you define your specific responsibilities?

What questions do you ask, regularly, where the answers have a direct impact on your area of responsibility?

Are there any questions that you ask today that go unanswered because of a lack of data or knowledge on how to use this data to answer those questions?

How often do you test theories, relative to your responsibilities, using business data?

What functions within your domain of responsibilities do you measure?

What data is collected on a regular basis within your domain of responsibility?

What systems used, within your domain of responsibility, store data? What data is stored?

Is the data collected and stored by your domain of responsibility shared with other domains within your organization?

Is data being collected by other domains of responsibility being shared with you today?

Do you suspect that there is data collected within other domains of responsibility that is not currently shared with you, but you feel would be helpful to your decision-making?

If you had access to all the data required today, what is one of your business challenges that you could better measure, manage, and improve immediately?

What do you get from asking these questions? The first question helps the stakeholder contain their thinking related to data to their domain of responsibility. All too often, when we start down the road of our data journey, we get side-tracked by the many temptations that present themselves to explore data that extends far beyond our immediate needs. This bogs down our projects. Focusing on our immediate needs help keep the project on-track, at the outset. The second question helps define the current state of business intelligence within the domain. The third question helps us to understand what is missing. The fourth question answers whether the area is doing more than simply reporting data. Is the business leader currently using data to drive decision-making? Then, what measurements are currently being taken?

From measuring, we move to data collection. Every domain collects data. It may not be collected in electronic format and it may not even be written down. It may become what is known as tribal knowledge, but it is still being collected. Is that data being shared? Often, business units collect data without any thought that the same data may be helpful to other business units in the organization. Finally, if the business leader had free access to all the data they needed, could they make better decisions? These questions start to build the inventory of data sources and begins to define how the data being collected may interact.

In addition to these questions, it is helpful to collect reporting specimens so that it can be understood how data is currently being used. It may also be required to employ the skills of an experienced interviewer who is able to help the stakeholders consider, deeply, the answers to their questions and draw out more detail than a cursory survey would.

Internal Clients

The next group of stakeholders consists of people within the organization impacted by the business decisions above. Why would their input be important if they are not ultimately responsible for making the decisions? These folks are often the best people to tell us why our decisions are bad and how they could be improved. Understanding their point of view, even if it is in error, will help us understand how to improve our decision-making with either better data or with increased transparency. I once had an employee who confessed that months earlier they had considered quitting their job because leadership (me) was failing to act on an issue that was impacting my internal clients (my staff). To me, the issue seemed insignificant; it was simply a matter of employee politics, if you will. The issue resolved itself as the problem employ self-selected themselves out (they quit). However, that result wasn't driven by a proactive business decision and if I hadn't gotten lucky (again), I could possibly have lost one or more of my really good employees. To my internal clients, it appeared as if I wasn't acting and was, therefore, an ineffective leader. I, on the other hand, didn't even see the problem. So, I was even worse a leader than they thought. Interviewing internal clients will help illuminate these types of hidden issues within the organization. The questions are somewhat similar, with some tweaks.

Define your specific job responsibilities?

What questions are you asked, regularly, where the answers come directly from your job responsibilities?

Are there any questions that you are asked today that go unanswered because of a lack of data or knowledge on how to use this data to answer those questions?

Are there processes in your job that seem inefficient or altogether useless?

What functions within your job scope are measured regularly?

What systems used, within your job function, store data? What data is stored?

Is the data collected and stored by your job function shared with other departments within your organization?

Is data being collected by other departments that is being shared with you today?

Do you suspect that there is data collected within other departments that is not currently shared with you, but you feel would be helpful to you in your job?

As you can see, these questions are tweaked somewhat to change the perspective, but are suggested to create the same type of results. You don't want to make a judgement of the value of answers at this point, but simply consider the full universe of data available and required for decisions to be made inside your organization.

External Clients

Finally, it can be informative to interview some external clients. Who are these people? It could be consumers of your products. Their needs and concerns may inspire you to consider data that you hadn't considered before. It could be vendors that you do business with. Do they have data that could be helpful to you, or is there information that you could provide to them that would make their product or service perform better? It could also be regulators, in some cases. How could data you provide to regulators help them more precisely understand your organizations operations? While external clients are often ignored in data strategies, one can see how the universe of potentially helpful data could be made even more extensive by including them.

Inventory and Map Data Sources

Based on the interviews conducted, you should have, at least, a foundational understanding of the data being collected by your organization from internal and external data sources. You will also understand some of the gaps in data and be able to determine how additional data sources might fulfill those data requirements. But a simple inventory is not sufficient for our strategy. We also need to map how the data may be integrated. It is the integration of data that makes it valuable at the enterprise level.

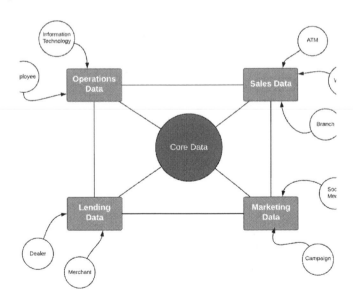

Above is a mind-map diagram depicting data sources that might be found in an organization like yours and how that data may be integrated. As you can see, this mapping of data sources could become very complex and there could be hundreds of ways that data could interact. Lending data could be integrated with operational data to study how lending decisions differ by educational level of the underwriter, integrating loan application data with employee profile data. Data regarding a recent marketing campaign is integrated with sales data to precisely measure the ROI on a given campaign. You can also see that some data, like ATM data, may consist of both internal and external datasets. Further, you begin to gain the understanding that without integration, this data exists in silos and is, most often, only used by the individuals in whose domain the data resides.

Define Key Performance Indicators

Key Performance indicators are the measurements we use to better understand how our business is working. You may be thinking that this is a simple process. In a lending environment, we are counting the number of loans originated, the total amount of loans originated, and the average amount of loans originated. You may also look at loan delinquency. In Marketing, you may look at campaign responses, retention/attrition rates, and cost-per-click. On the operational side, you may monitor branch activity, transaction error rates, and call-center traffic. These are very common and practical measurements, but they may not always provide a clear and accurate picture of your business's health. Let's look at delinquent loans, for example. We may ask what a healthy delinquency ratio should be. The fact of the matter is, there is no magic number.

117

Therefore, we must define our indicators in the context of our world. For instance, how does our loan delinquency compare to all other financial institutions. Is our delinquency rising while other organization's delinquency is falling? In other words, are there comparative benchmarks that can be used to help build more informative KPI's. For example, using data from other financial institutions, we could determine what percentile our delinquency is in. Are we in the 50th percentile or are we in the 90th percentile.

Once there is more access to data, more sophisticated data can be used to build more informative dimensional measurements. Today, we count the number of credit applications that we take and then count the number of loan applications that are funded as loans. This gives a pull-through rate. In other words, we can say that our baseline pull-through rate is a certain percentage of applications. If the pull-through rises, we believe we are doing better. If it is lowered, then we believe we are performing poorly. But what if we added risk as a dimension? Let's say that our average pull through rate is 50% where one of every two credit applications ultimately results in a funded loan. What if the pull-through rate of high-risk loans is 80% and the pull-through rate of low-risk loans is only 10%? It may be perfectly okay that your financial institution is better at originating high-risk loans than low-risk loans, but what if it isn't? Without the dimensional data, there would be no way to know where you stand.

You may be saying to yourself at this point, this seems awfully simplistic, even with dimensional data. If this is true for you and you have access to this level of information already, I applaud you. However, I've worked with dozens of credit unions that do not. They know they need it and can articulate why, but that have not yet figured out how to get access to this level of data on a regular basis. I've even worked with non-financial services entities that cannot tell you, at any given moment, how many customers they serve and for how long they have served them. Perhaps we revel in bemoaning our lack of business intelligence, but I'm hopeful it is just a matter of creating better strategies to produce it.

Define Short-, Medium-, and Long-Term Goals

You may be familiar with setting goals and even short-term and long-term goals, but I've found that medium-term goals are also necessary for EDDCT Strategies. There are two reasons for this. One reason is that technology changes so quickly that it is necessary to set more frequent gates for progress and some technology required to fully meet your objective may not be fully developed when your strategy is created. A second reason is what I would call a data-literacy deficiency. Generally, short-term goals are those goals that can or should be achieved in twelve months or less. Long-term goals are expected to be accomplished over three to five years. A short-term goal might be to fully staff the organization over the period of twelve months. A long-term goal might be to reduce the turn-over rate of employees to less than 10% in three years. On a data journey, however, you will find that there are some very foundational issues that you must address in the short-term, requiring some of your short-term goals related to using data to be pushed out over twelve months. But, these goals need to be accomplished within 18 to 24 months, not three to five years. This gives us an intermediate tranche for goal setting. If you have a data-literacy deficiency, you may strongly consider medium-term goals in your strategy.

Here are some potential short-term goals that you may consider in your organization:

1. **Create Data Governance and Engagement (EDGE) Team** – most small and medium-sized financial organizations do not yet have a Chief Data Officer who is empowered to govern the organization's data resources. In these organizations, it may be better to form a cross-functional team that shares the responsibilities of governance and engagement. I like to call them EDGE Teams and charge them with both data governance and *engagement*.

2. **Create a Centralized Data Store** – often described as a data warehouse, or data lake, it is a resource where data is gathered, integrated, and stored in a format that is accessible to business users for decision-making. It is clear why this goal must supersede goals related to using data in practice, but it is a time-consuming process that requires extreme focus and attention. Don't let the names fool you. A Data Warehouse doesn't have to be large and complex to meet the definition.

3. **Defining Facts, Measures, Metrics and Dimensions** – this goal goes beyond simply looking at the organizations Key Performance Indicators and begins to define the elements of descriptive, predictive, and prescriptive analytics. This part of the strategy may

require help from third parties, like outside data transformation consultants.

4. **Creation of KPI Dashboards** – these simple dashboards would represent the first step toward data visualization. It is the low-hanging fruit based on the KPI's identified in the prior step. But, it provides some immediate results that satisfy the organization's thirst for ROI. In other words, gain early wins to keep stakeholders happy as you work on some of the more difficult goals to attain.

Here are some potential medium-term goals that you may consider in your organization:

1. **Using Data to Better Allocate Resources** – Often organizations will add production requirements to existing resources as if it is a zero-sum game. Information Technology resources often fall victim to this paradigm. As the organization adds recent technology, they simply add the workload to the existing resources without evaluating the impact on efficacy. Using production and efficiency measurements to inform resource allocation helps the organization to properly assess the impact of its decision-making.

2. **Fostering a Data-Driven Culture** – This is indicative of a maturing organization where data isn't a convenience, but a necessity. Expectations for the use of data are documented and a defined decision-making process is enforced. Employees are trained to use data in decision-making and job descriptions incorporate data literacy requirements.

3. **Developing Augmented Intelligence Resources** – Augmented Intelligence is the practice of serving up data to assist decision-makers in real-time. Unlike Artificial Intelligence which promises to overtake human reasoning and decision-making, Augmented Intelligence equips decision-makers with better information to assist in human decision-making. A good example of Augmented Intelligence would be The RiskGenie by CMRG Solutions. The software provides loan underwriters with real-time risk assessments of a loan application as information is changed during the lending process that may affect the risk of the loan.

Finally, here are some possible long-term goals:

1. **Fully Transformed Data Culture** – This would represent the conclusion of the development stage of the strategy and the jumping off point for intuitively implementing data processes and applications as a regular practice.

2. **Predictive Analytics** – Analytics that predict future performance based on historical data. Using predictive analytics, predictive models are employed to predict performance based on significant variable inputs. This data takes time to develop, test and implement. For this reason, they are appropriately considered long-term goals.

3. **Prescriptive Analytics** – Like Predictive Analytics, Prescriptive Analytics rely on historical data and predictive models but elevate the value of the data one additional layer in providing a prescribed solution. If the data shows an unhealthy rise in risk or external

forces that will have a deleterious impact on performance, prescriptive models will recommend corrective actions. In other words, if this happens, do this.

Publish and Socialize Roadmap

Often overlooked, publishing and socializing the organizations roadmap for its data journey serves, at least, a couple of purposes. The first purpose is one of accountability. By publishing and socializing the roadmap, leadership is signaling its commitment to change. It's hard to back away from something that you told everyone you would do. This shouldn't be taken lightly as I would say that a reluctance to publish and socialize the roadmap signals a lack of commitment for the same reason. The second purpose for publication and socialization, is to calm the masses. When word gets out that the organization is pursuing a data transformation, everyone, of course, wants their data projects completed first. A seemingly unreasonable delay causes them to believe that their project isn't even going to be worked on. A roadmap solves this problem as it creates a visualization of the organization's priorities and helps stakeholders in the organization to understand the timing of when their project will be completed.

****

There you have it; a framework for creating an Enterprise Data-Driven Culture Transformation Strategy. It seems simple but should not be assumed or ignored. The process *is* the product more so than the strategy document itself, as the process mines and brings awareness to opportunities. Beginning without this important process of mining this resident knowlege could potentially leave opportunities undiscovered.

Chapter 7

Data Integration and Modeling: Part I, Definition of Important Terms

Integrating and modeling data can be complex and time-consuming, but it doesn't have to keep your organization from beginning its transformation journey. I believe the fear of the complexities that could be involved have kept many of my financial institution clients from undertaking the task. The result of delaying this process is that data resides in constrained boxes, or silos, throughout your organization. You have customer or member data in one box and transaction account data in another. Customer service statistics are managed by the call-center manager, and sale statistics are managed by the business development manager. Attempting to integrate the data for analysis becomes problematic without a well-planned strategy.

Not only is there an issue of data residing in different domains within the organization, there are logical questions that must be answered about how data should be used for decision-making. For example, let's say that you are trying to analyze deposit account behavior by age of the account-owner. It is a simple task if all accounts have a single owner, because you can simply categorize the accounts into age groups based on that owner's age. But, what if there are two individuals listed as account owners who are of different ages? Or, what if you have a non-person entity as an account owner combined with a real-person account owner? These are the types of questions that arise in data analytics that lead to the development of business rules that are used to define how data is integrated and to develop data models. It is outside the scope of this book to settle every question related to data integration and modeling as it may pertain to your organization, but I will attempt to visit a few of the most common issues and questions that have arisen among my credit union clients.

Data Integration

What does it mean to integrate data? Quite simply, it means to join data elements from disparate datasets into a single data model. We are so accustomed, in business, to working with flat tables, especially those that can be wrangled into an Excel® spreadsheet. Some of us may even be able to join worksheets in the same workbook using unique identifiers with a one-to-one relationship, like a look-up table, for instance, where you look up the price of an item for sale. But, how would we join data of different complexities or velocities? In the example above, you have a single account with two account owners. This type of account has a higher level of complexity than a single-owner account because it represents a one-to-many relationship instead of a simple one-to-one relationship. Data velocity comes into play when you compare account data from an account table, for instance, and transaction data from a transaction table. An account is created once, at a single moment in time. An account transaction is created every time a transaction is made on an account. But, an account is not created every time a transaction is logged. While these data can be integrated, they do not have the same velocity. Integrating data requires the understanding of both the complexity and velocity of data and how to synchronize them.

Data Modeling is the discipline used to strategize and diagram how data will be integrated together based on business requirements so that developers and business users can understand how data is related and integrated. A complete data model consists of, at least, three important components; a conceptual data model, a physical data model and the data itself. Conceptual Data Models are often depicted as Entity Relationship Diagrams (ERD), illustrating, in most cases, a relational database where related data tables are linked together by common fields. Certainly, there are several diverse ways of designing a database, data warehouse or data lake described later in this book, but for simplicity's sake our discussion in this book will be primarily related to the relational data base model, not the design of the facility, as there are many texts available on database architecture. The purpose of this book is to only familiarize the reader with the general concepts. For credit unions companies, there are some specific challenges that will be encountered when working on data integration and modeling and it is important for business users to understand these challenges as they participate in transforming to a data-driven decision culture.

Before we dig too deep into integration and modeling, it may be helpful to cover some terms that are often used in data environments that are not always clearly understood by business users. This doesn't mean that business users are not intelligent or are uninformed, but they represent a language that is not commonly used in most business environments. The trouble is, when these terms are not understood, or are not used properly, it can create confusion among project participants, slowing or even killing a data project. Further, vendors may attempt to capitalize on your organization's lack of understanding or confusion and you may end up investing in technology that you will not use or that will not meet the requirements of your project.

Data

Data can exist in many forms, continuous and categorical, text and numeric, and/or structured and unstructured. Data is simply all the facts, measures and dimensions collected to perform various personal and business functions. Data, in its raw form, does not constitute information, however. For example, most databases store descriptive facts as codes, like an account type code, which are not easily discernable by a business user. Your organization may use a loan type description of 'Used Auto Loan' that is represented in a data table with a numeric code, like '100023'. Unless you have a reference table handy, the numeric code may not be easily translated into a name or term that you can understand. Data often must be translated into easily understood information to be used in decision-making.

Data Tables

Data tables are used in a database to store data. Tables are made up of rows and columns. Most commonly, each row in a data table represents a data record, like a single loan account for example, and the table columns represent fields in that record where data is stored, like Account Number, Account Balance, etc. A spreadsheet is the best visual comparison to a data table in a database and, in fact, an Excel® worksheet or worksheet region can be used as a data table in a database. Data tables are sometimes referred to as 'Entities'. An Entity Relationship Diagram (ERD), referenced above, is a visual representation of data tables in a database and how those tables may be related to one another (See Appendix I).

Database

A database is a collection of one or more data tables or entities. Data tables in a database may or may not be related but, typically, data in a single database is loosely related. For example, you may have a customer relationship management database that includes data related to prospective customers, current customers, and sales statistics or a transaction database which stores data about deposits, withdrawals, and loan payments. There are several types of databases including flat and relational databases. A flat database is one where there is either a single table or, if there is more than one table, there is no relationship between the tables. In a relational database, data tables are highly related. For example, in a flat database you may have an account data table that contains all the information about an account, including all the account owner information. When retrieving data from a flat database, you would typically query a single data table. In a relational database, you might have an account table and an account owner table. The account table would contain data related only to the account and perhaps a single field that identifies an account owner, but not all the account owner information, as in the single-table, flat database. The account owner table would then be linked to the account table using the account owner identification field as a common identifier. This is an important distinction to understand, as many core data processing systems and loan origination systems use flat databases for storage, or at least only allow extracts from their central data store in a single flat data table. On the other hand, your central data repository, or data warehouse, will likely be a relational database.

Data Warehouse or Data Mart

A data warehouse is a type of database, described above, constructed to be specifically used for business intelligence or data analytics. There are several ways to build data warehouses and many design theories to improve capabilities and performance, but it is important to understand that if the design does not support easy and efficient access by business users for decision making, it is not, technically, a data warehouse. Often, business leaders are confused by what a data warehouse is because the term warehouse infers that the definition has to do with size. Warehouses are typically large in the real world, but they are also organized for a purpose. It is the organization of the data warehouse database that we

130

should focus on in the context of business intelligence, not necessarily the size.

Data archives are not data warehouses even if they are large because they do not fit the defined purpose of a data warehouse. Archives do store large volumes of data and often in an organized manner to facilitate disaster recovery, but they do not provide easy access to business users to be used in decision-making. If I were to compare data in different forms to serving a meal, core data would be what I would call stove-top servings, archive data would be frozen food and a data warehouse would be a buffet. Data that is stored in the core has a limited shelf-life and is present for specific operational purposes, like a single meal prepared on a stove-top. Once the transaction (meal) is over, the data (food) is rarely needed again. Archived data, or data that is transferred from the core system to permanent storage is like freezing leftover food. You may or may not need it in the future, but you want to store it just in case. Retrieving food from a freezer requires that it be thawed and re-heated to eat. Archived data usually requires a great deal of work to make it accessible for any purpose, much less freely accessible for analytics. However, a data warehouse allows data to be ready for use at any time based on a business user's need, like a buffet typically has a variety of food kept warm so that diners can take what they want, when they want it.

Sometimes, data warehouses are referred to as data marts. A data mart is like a data warehouse, with the distinction that data warehouse typically describes an enterprise data store where data is collected and integrated across the organization and a data mart is constructed to serve the needs of a specific business discipline, such as Marketing or Lending.

Data Lake

Becoming more popular to discuss, especially in Artificial Intelligence, a data lake consists of substantial amounts of, often unrelated, data in raw form. The term is often used in conjunction with 'Big Data' which consists of data both in and outside the domain of an organization. An example of a data lake used by financial institutions would be if your organization was collecting data, not only from your own organization, but consumer data from social media platforms, financial data from financial websites, etc., and that data remained in its raw format, untranslated for business users to use in decision-making. Presumably, you would mine this data for experimentation and research before consuming it into your data warehouse.

Extract, Transform and Load (ETL)

While discussing data projects, the term ETL will most definitely be used by the more technical resources on your team. An ETL process describes the way data will be extracted from one data source, like a core data processing system, transformed into information, and then loaded into a data repository such as a database, data warehouse, or data mart. ETL's often encompass the business logic that defines how raw data is translated into information that business users can use. For example, let's say you want to store the age of an account owner in your data warehouse, but your data processing system only stores the account owner's birthdate. The ETL process would define how that birthdate would be transformed into an age. In this case, you might want the account owner age at the time the account was opened, you may want the current age, or you may want both. This would require to different calculations, one calculating the years between the account owner's birthdate and the account opening date, and one calculating the years between the account owner's birthdate and the current data. You may also want your ETL to assign the account owner to an age group defined by a range of ages. These are the type of discussions that take place during the planning stage.

****

The four most common terms used in Business Intelligence are 'Fact' or 'Measure', 'Metric' and 'Dimension'. These four terms, which define data types, are foundational to understanding how data should be integrated and modeled. Understanding the purpose of and differences between the four is of utmost importance when beginning the process of modeling data. Failure to gain this understanding is they key reason why so many data projects encounter issues that either delay deployment of data driven decision-making or result in abandonment of the project altogether. Allow me to define these four terms as it will help as we continue through the next couple of chapters ahead.

Facts or Measures

A data fact is just what it says, it is a fact about your business that is gathered during a business process. There are dimensional facts and there are measure facts. Dimensional facts are used to qualify data. The 'accountID' is considered a

133

dimensional fact and is non-additive. You cannot add it to anything. It describes the data record by indicating which account generated the facts. Measures are numeric values, typically additive, that appear in a fact table as seen in our ERD illustration in Appendix I. An 'Account Balance' is a measure. It can be summed or added to something else to create a metric, so it is additive. An Account Balance, in and of itself, tells us nothing about the account but only the account balance. A dimensional fact would help describe what type of account it is, like an account code, for example.

Another measure fact might be a deposit account balance. These are not counts or totals, simply measures that are drawn from a single data snapshot. For example, if you take a snapshot of deposit accounts on the first day of a statement cycle, the balance may be $1,000. If you take a snapshot on the second day of the cycle, the balance on the account might be $2,000, after a direct deposit is received. Both daily balances are fact measures. Facts are 'atomic-level' data and, ideally, do not include averages, counts, sums or any other type of aggregation. 'Atomic-level' data is data that exists in a database at its most granular level.

The table below demonstrates how facts can be either dimensions or measures. Even though a dimension may be a numeric value, it is used to provide a qualitative value to a record. It is not additive as it cannot be used in a calculation. Measures are quantitative and additive.

Facts				
Dimension	Dimension	Dimension	Measure	Measure
Account_ID	Date_ID	Trans_ID	Trans_Amt	Balance
1000123	20181231	911111	$25.00	$10,025

There is some confusion on this topic, even among Data Scientist. The confusion is rooted in the diverse types of data warehouses that can be used. If you are using MOLAP, or a multi-dimensional data cube, measures are often pre-aggregated or summarized for every dimension. They appear much like a metric as defined below, so they are not technically found at their most granular level. If you are using ROLAP, or a relational database, like a star-schema, measures are not pre-aggregated, so the original definition holds true.

Metrics

Sometimes confusing because we use terms like measure and metric interchangeably in the real world, metrics, in the business intelligence nomenclature, are the calculations of Facts or Measures that form our Key Performance Indicators (KPI). Using our Account Balance fact above, we may create a metric called 'Total Account Balances' or 'Sum of Account Balances' which represents the total of all account balances in a data snapshot, or a total of all the rows in a single column of a data table. Let's say we have 100 accounts in our snapshot and they each have an account balance of $1,000. The value of our Sum of Account Balances metric would be $100 thousand (100 x 1,000). In the same way, we could average the account balances and create a metric we call 'Average Account Balance', which in this case would be $1,000 ($100,000 / 100). One can typically identify a metric by leading terms such as average, total, count and so forth.

Often, financial institutions must 'weight' metrics to make them more meaningful, such as a Weighted Average Rate. When weighting a metric, you must choose another related fact that provides an appropriate weight for weighting the measure to be weighted. Let's say you are trying to obtain an average interest rate in your account data table to project income in the future. You could simply calculate an average on the Interest Rate column or field for all records in the table, but this would not take into consideration the amount deposited into each account which might skew your projected income. To overcome this, you would create a new column in your data table that stores the product of the Account Balance and the Interest Rate ($1,000 * 0.58% = 5800%). This would be your Rate Weighting fact, or measure, weighted by the account balance. Now, instead of simply taking an average of the Interest Rate data field and multiplying it by the total balances in the table, you would divide the sum of the Rate Weighting column by the sum of the Account Balance field to find your Weighted Average Rate and then multiply that value by the total balances in the table.

Simple Average Rate

Account #	Balance	Rate
100023	$10,000	0.25%
100024	$1,000	0.75%
100025	$2,500	0.35%
100026	$5,000	0.50%
Average Rate		**0.46%**

Weighted Average Rate

Account #	Balance	Rate	Rate Weighting
100023	$10,000	0.25%	2500%
100024	$1,000	0.75%	750%
100025	$2,500	0.35%	875%
100026	$5,000	0.50%	2500%
	$18,500		6625%
Weighted Average Rate			**0.36%**

As you can see, there is a significant difference in the resulting rate *metrics.* The difference is because the accounts with higher interest rates have lower balances and vice versa. Again, we created the weighted metric by adding a fact column in the data table that represented a weighted value of a raw fact, or measure. The reason you would want to create weighted facts in your data is to measure values more accurately. For example, if I use the simple average rate, above, to project income, I would over-state the result. In this case, I would multiply 0.46% against the total balances of $18,500 and come up with a projected income of $85.10. But, if I calculated the projected income for each record, independently, I would only come up with $66.25. That is variance of 28.5%, which is significant. Using the Weighted Average Rate metric instead, created by using the Rate Weighting measure, gives me the same result as if I calculated each record individually.

From the Weighted Average Rate table above:

$$\$18,500 \times 0.0036 = \$66.25$$

Calculating projected income on each record:

Account #	Balance	Rate	Income
100023	$10,000	0.25%	$25.00
100024	$1,000	0.75%	$7.50
100025	$2,500	0.35%	$8.75
100026	$5,000	0.50%	$25.00
Projected Income			**$66.25**

I should pause at this point and say that many current analytics software platforms contribute to the confusion of these definitions, and perhaps, will require that we change the language going forward, at some point. Many analytics platforms seemingly describe metrics as measures. Microsoft's Power BI software, for example, has a feature that allows you to 'create a new column' (measure) in a data table based on a calculation of two existing facts or measures, as was demonstrated above. I referred to this, previously, as creating a new measure, but Power BI does not refer to this activity in the same way. On the other hand, Power BI's 'New Measure' feature allows you to create a metric based on a calculation of two aggregations of existing facts, or metrics. The reason for the seeming conflict is, most probably, due the use of the MDX language associated with Online Analytical Processing (OLAP). With OLAP, aggregations are pre-summarized by dimensional data, so measures at the record level of granularity are not as prevalent as   they are in a relational database.

138

Dimensions

Dimensional data is descriptive and provides a means for categorization. For example, the Sum of Account Balances metric above is not descriptive. It doesn't tell you whether the balances are from a loan account or a deposit account. If it is a loan account, it doesn't tell you what type of loan it is, the term of the loan, or who originated the loan. Dimensional data provides a qualitative value and grouping mechanism. Dimensions allow us to categorize information so that it makes sense to us from a business perspective.

Looking at our definition of Facts or Measures, note the scenario using daily balances. On the first day of a statement cycle, the account had a balance of $1,000. On the second day of the cycle, the account had a balance of $2,000. If you simply created a metric for the 'Sum of Account Balances', this metric would give you a result of $3,000. For this one account, it would calculate all records with no categorization. In other words, it would be adding the account balance for each daily snapshot in the database but not grouping the metric by snapshot date. This, likely, wouldn't give you the information you are looking for. You are either looking for the total balance of all accounts on a single day or the average balance of accounts over a series of snapshots, such as an 'Average Daily Balance'. In this type of scenario, the date of the snapshot would be a useful *dimension to* slice or filter the results.

I consider the snapshot date dimension to be an *organic* dimension in databases because it is existential. Without a data snapshot, there is no data. Without a snapshot date, there is no snapshot. Every record in the database has, at least, a snapshot date. It may be implied if there is only one snapshot, but two snapshots cannot properly exist in a single data file without a snapshot date dimension. Organic dimensions are those that exist because the record exists.

It is likely, however, that there are many dates that can be associated with a data record. In the case of an account, you have the date the account was created, you have the date of an account snapshot, and you have the date of the last transaction on an account, to name just a few. So, following along with our example above, we could use dimensions to give us the Sum of Account Balances on a particular date, view the Sum of Account Balances over a time-series using the snapshot date dimension, or calculate the Average Account Balance of an account over a number of snapshots.

Other dimensions can be *derived* from organic dimensions, fact data in a data record, or facts in a table related to a record. For example, is a loan delinquent, yes or no? Typically, there is not an organic dimension in a data record that explicitly classifies a loan as delinquent or not delinquent. Therefore, you must derive the dimension from available fact data. Based on your requirements for measuring delinquency, you would identify data fields that would help create the desired dimension. Loan records typically have a 'Days Delinquent' fact data field, but you wouldn't want to use this as a dimension because it would group all loans with zero days delinquent together and then aggregate by delinquent days, such as 1, 2, 3, …, 30. Instead, there is typically a threshold where delinquency matters to the business user, like at 30 days or more. A derived dimension would then look at the Days Delinquent field and group loans as delinquent (yes) where the Days Delinquent are 30 or more days and not delinquent (no) where the Days Delinquent are less than 30 days.

Some of the software solutions that will be reviewed in Chapter 10 allow for this type of grouping of organic dimensions, such as Days Delinquent, on the fly. However, I prefer having enterprise level derived dimensions so that there is no confusion within in the organization on how data is grouped.

Loan Portfolio Data

Account	Days Delinquent	Amount
Loan 1	0	$5,000
Loan 2	10	$5,000
Loan 3	0	$5,000
Loan 4	15	$5,000
Loan 5	31	$5,000
Loan 6	45	$5,000
Loan 7	60	$5,000
Loan 8	0	$5,000
Loan 9	10	$5,000
Loan 10	20	$5,000

Organic Dimension Aggregation

Days Delinquent	Amount
0	$15,000
10	$10,000
15	$5,000
20	$5,000
31	$5,000
45	$5,000
60	$5,000
Grand Total	**$50,000**

Derived Dimension Aggregation

Delinquent	Amount
No	$35,000
Yes	$15,000
Grand Total	**$50,000**

In the next chapter, we will continue our discussion of data integration and modeling by looking at some of the considerations that organizations should make when integrating and modeling data.

Chapter 8

Data Integration and Modeling: Part II, Important Considerations

I've gone through the process of providing the explanation of key terms in the prior chapter because it is likely that everyday business users will not understand how important these foundational components are in constructing a 'single source of truth' data repository. However, if you do understand how these components work together, your team can work to build a more accurate and efficient data resource. What typically happens, however, is that a business user or decision-maker will provide a very vague or ambiguous request for a metric or KPI. For example, the Chief Lending Officer will ask for a count of loans. The data analysist will go back to the core data processor and extract data related to loans from the system database and create a report showing the count of loans as of the day the request was made. When the CLO receives the data, she is frustrated because the numbers are way higher than what she is expecting.

So, the she asks the analyst what data was extracted. The analyst explains that she ran a query on the core database for all existing loan accounts, which is technically what was requested. Of course, this included loans and lines of credit with zero-balances. The CLO refines her request and says, "exclude the zero-balance accounts". The analyst's new report now has a KPI that seems too low. The CLO is now exasperated, wondering why the analyst can't simply provide a count of 'existing' loans. Of course, when the analyst excluded zero-balance accounts, she eliminated all active lines of credit that did not have a balance, which is not a business requirement for lines of credit to 'exist' or remain 'open'. This scenario happens every day in financial institutions across the U.S. It's not a problem of intelligence, it's an issue of poor planning, modeling, and communication.

Let's take a quick look at this dilemma in a little more detail. The chart below shows data that could exist in a typical credit union database.

Account Type	Account Status	Account Balance
Loan	Active	$10,000
Loan	Inactive	$0
Credit Line	Active	$5,000
Credit Line	Active	$0
Credit Line	Inactive	$0
Credit Line	Active	-$100
Credit Line	Inactive	$2,000

Considering the table above, let's try and answer the CLO's question as originally stated. The CLO wanted a count of all loan accounts. The above table shows seven loan accounts with different balances and status. Some are 'Active' and some are 'Inactive'. Some have positive balances, some have $0 balances and one has a negative balance. But, the answer to the original question asked by the CLO, without any presumption, is seven.

Let's say, however, that the analyst goes a step further and presumes that that the CLO is looking for loans that are active only. The answer to that question, based on the data above, is only four. Or, say the analyst presumes the CLO is looking for loans where the balance is greater than $0. The answer is also four but includes one Inactive account with a balance of $2,000 and excludes and Active account with a $0 balance. What the CLO wants, however, is a count of all loans that are either Active or Inactive with a balance not equal to $0. Our raw loan data does not provide this information, so we must construct a 'Measure' in our database to accommodate this business requirement. The table below includes an additional column (measure), Loan Count, that is built off a business rule that requires that a loan should be counted if it is active, regardless of balance, OR has a balance other than $0. In other words, the loans status is not fully resolved or closed.

Account Type	Account Status	Account Balance	Loan Count
Installment Loan	Active	$10,000	1
Installment Loan	Inactive	$0	0
Credit Line	Active	$5,000	1
Credit Line	Active	$0	1
Credit Line	Inactive	$0	0
Credit Line	Active	-$100	1
Credit Line	Inactive	$2,000	1

With this new measure in place, we can now create a metric, Count of Loans by adding all the values in the Loan Count Column. This is now a metric that can be used throughout the organization that has an agreed upon definition based on a clearly stated business rule. This defined metric can be sliced or filtered using dimensional data to further analyze the information. In this case, the dimensions we can use, often text-based, are Account Type and Account Status. Using these dimensions and metrics, it is simple to create a pivot table, like the one below, that shows the correct answer, 5, and answers to some additional questions that were not asked.

	Active	Inactive	Grand Total
Credit Line	3	1	4
Installment Loan	1	0	1
Grand Total	**4**	**1**	**5**

The pivot table above provides a higher level of visualization to the business user than simply providing them with a count. In this case, the CLO can now also see that there is a total of five loans that meet the metric requirements, four are lines of credit and one is an installment loan. Four of the loans that meet the metric requirement are Active and one is Inactive. If the business user wants to only see the active accounts that meet the requirements, he or she would simply filter the table, including only Active Accounts, as demonstrated in the table below.

	Active	Grand Total
Credit Line	3	3
Loan	1	1
Grand Total	**4**	**4**

In this case, by filtering the data for just the Active accounts that meet the metric definition, the new answer becomes four instead of five. Keep in mind that we are still working with the same metric we defined as loans that are either active or have an outstanding balance. We did not have to build a new metric to accommodate the reporting change, we only changed the slicing or filtering of data by dimension.

All too often, however, business users will write fact and measure requirements that are too specific, and these measures will be 'hard-coded' in the central data repository. What tends to happen when this is allowed is that there is confusion over what the metric requirements are, or when the business requirements change, the metric breaks. For example, you may encounter a request for a metric for the number of borrowers in zip code 75001 called 'Target Borrowers'. The database administrator then builds an ETL process that adds a record to the Target Borrower fact table in the database with the count of borrowers in the target zip code every time a snapshot is saved. Then the postal service comes and splits the defined zip code in two, assigning half of the residents of the 75001 zip code to a new zip code, 75002. The trouble is, no one remembers to update the logic in the ETL code that creates that target group fact table every time a snapshot is run. Suddenly, your count of targeted borrowers is reduced by half and no one knows why. You could go back and correct the issue by writing new code in the ETL and rebuilding your fact table from day one with the new parameters, but that is inefficient and prone to error. Instead, you would include a borrower count measure and slice or filter your data by the Zip Code dimension which would include all zip codes. This would allow you to select one or multiple zip codes to include in the Target Borrowers group and change the group as your definition changes in the future.

I always like to remind my clients and customers that there is only one way to count 'Borrowers'. A person is a borrower, or they are not a borrower. One shouldn't try to over-specify what the definition of a particular characteristic is. As an organization, you need to define how a borrower should be counted. Once that definition is established, you can use dimensional data such as zip code, date, state, county, etc. to slice and filter your count of borrowers until you arrive at the information you are seeking. Embedding dimensional data into metric or measure definitions makes the database inefficient and, again, makes it prone to error or confusion.

I had a similar circumstance arise at a non-financial institution client and it nearly became insurmountable. The primary reason was that the client couldn't grasp this concept of metrics and dimensions. In this case, the client wanted to count 'customers', but the issue was they had entities included in their list of 'customers' with considerably diverse types of relationships. For example, they had contracted customers who were paying them monthly for a single product. They also had 'indirect' customers who had access to one or more products but were contracted *indirectly* through a third-party provider, so they were not paying and were not contracted directly with my client. Then, there were customers with separate contracts for multiple products who were paying monthly. They also had customers who had purchased a single-use product and had paid only one time but had no continuing relationship. There were customers with contracts but, for whatever reason, the customer was not required to pay anything. Finally, there were customers who had been under contract in the past, but the contract had now been cancelled. On any given day, based on who you asked, you might get dozens of different answers in response to the question, "how many customers you have?" This was very frustrating for the organization's leadership.

There is really only one answer to the above question and it is equivalent to how many customer account records are in the database. Dimensional data then helps to categorize the account metric into specific groups for analysis. The existence of an account record creates an organic dimension for whether an account has ever existed. The dimension used to answer the question of whether an account is a current account is derived by the status of the account to determine if it is 'open' or 'closed'. Does the account have a contract? If not, then the account is indirect, versus a direct account that has a contract. Has an account contracted for one product or multiple products, etc., etc. Below is a data table depicting a scenario like the one above with granularity at the product level. In other words, customers with multiple products are counted more than once. For example, Customer 2 has two products and would be counted twice.

Account	Contract	Product	Status	Paying
Customer 1	Yes	Product 1	Open	Yes
Customer 2	No	Product 1	Closed	No
Customer 2	Yes	Product 2	Open	Yes
Customer 3	Yes	Product 1	Open	No
Customer 3	Yes	Product 3	Open	Yes
Customer 4	No	Product 1	Open	No
Customer 4	No	Product 2	Closed	No
Customer 5	Yes	Product 1	Closed	No
Customer 6	No	Product 1	Open	No
Customer 7	Yes	Product 1	Closed	No
Customer 8	No	Product 1	Closed	No
Customer 9	Yes	Product 1	Open	Yes
Customer 10	No	Product 1	Open	No

Pivot Table of Product Account Relationships

| | | Account Status | | | | |
| | | Closed | | Open | | |
Contract	Product	Not Paying	Paying	Not Paying	Paying	Total
No	Product 1	2		3		5
No	Product 2	1				1
	Subtotal	*3*	*0*	*3*	*0*	*6*
Yes	Product 1	2		1	2	5
Yes	Product 2				1	1
Yes	Product 3				1	1
	Subtotal	*2*	*0*	*1*	*4*	*7*
	Total	5	0	4	4	13

In the table above, a single metric is used, the Count of Accounts, where an account is defined as a single client/product pair. If you want to know how many total accounts have been served by your products, the answer is a total of 13. You can see this total matches the total number of records in the data table. If you want to know how many clients are currently being served by all products, the answer is 8 open accounts, 4 paying accounts and 4 non-paying accounts. If you wanted to know how many indirect, non-contracted and non-paying accounts you have, the answer is 3.

The above table goes down to the product granularity. So, if a customer has more than one product they will be counted multiple times. Perhaps, you only want to count single entities once, regardless of the number of products they have used. In this case, you would need to decide how you want to handle the possible different contract and product statuses. The table below shows what the account data table might look like if we raise the granularity to the customer level, rather than the product level.

Account	Contract	Status	Paying
Customer 1	Yes	Open	Yes
Customer 2	Yes	Open	Yes
Customer 3	Yes	Open	No
Customer 4	No	Open	No
Customer 5	Yes	Open	No
Customer 6	No	Open	No
Customer 7	Yes	Closed	No
Customer 8	No	Closed	No
Customer 9	Yes	Open	Yes
Customer 10	No	Open	No

In this case, we had to determine how we would classify customers if they had multiple product accounts. What if they have had contracts on two products but one is open and the other closed? Or, what if they are paying for one product and not the other. To create the table above, it was determined that if they had at least one contract for a product, then the contract classification would be 'yes'. If there was at least one open product contract, then the status would be 'open'. Finally, if they were paying for at least one product, then they would be classified as 'paying'.

Pivot Table of Account Relationships

Contract	Account Status				
	Closed		Open		
	Not Paying	Paying	Not Paying	Paying	Total
No	1		3	0	4
Yes	1		2	3	6
Total	2	0	5	3	10

Again, we are still using only one metric, Count of Accounts. All we have done is changed the dimension definitions. In this case, we have served 10 customers total. Eight customer accounts are still open with at least one product and two are closed. Six of the accounts have contracts for at least one product and four do not have contracts for any products. If I wanted to know how many direct, paying customers I currently have, the answer is 3. That is, there are three accounts with at least one product contract where the account is currently open, and the customer is currently paying.

This is how multi-dimensional data analytics is supposed to work. It is not necessary to build logic for hundreds of metrics, but rather use dimensional data to filter and slice metrics so that you arrive at the answer you are looking for but not necessarily eliminate other possible answers. Understanding these principles are key to successfully building a 'single source of the truth' data repository. Misunderstanding these principles is the single most prevalent reason why organization's data integration and modeling projects stall or fail. As we continue, I will address some of the other common issues that credit   unions encounter.

Bad or Missing Data

One of the most difficult shifts for credit unions is viewing their data for something other than accounting purposes. Credit unions have a long history of tracking debits and credits, accurate reporting and protecting account integrity. Financial services leaders often see data in a different light than Data Scientists do. Data Scientists know that you can sample data for analytics purposes; you don't have to view the entire dataset to conduct analysis. Data Scientists view data in large sets of similarly categorized records where financial services managers tend to concentrate on a single account record. A Data Scientist can show you a group of accounts that could potentially cause a loss, where managers want to know exactly who it is that has or will cause a loss. Finally, credit union leaders are entrenched in tried and true banking paradigms, mostly related to eliminating risk, where Data Scientists will focus on challenging current paradigms and seeking opportunities to increase margins by understanding, managing, and pricing risk. These conflicts can create roadblocks to creating a data-driven decision culture.

A good example of how this plays out in the real world is when analysts encounter bad or missing data. The simplest way to work around outliers in data sets is to eliminate them from the analysis. If a data record has missing or obviously bad data, simply exclude it. There is rarely enough of them to make a significant difference in the analysis. However, when working in and with financial institutions, there is a mindset that the bottom line numbers must match up. Obviously, if you eliminate a record from your analysis the total balance of accounts, for example, will not match what is on record in the financial institution's general ledger. While I've personally tried to overcome this hurdle with what I believed to be sound reason, I have lost nearly every battle on this point with my clients. Therefore, I find it now more productive to search for ways to accommodate the irregularities in a record than try and eliminate the record altogether.

Here is a prime example of what I'm describing. Take the loan-to-value (LTV) of a collateralized loan. Many times, when I receive data for analysis from a financial institution it will have LTV's that make absolutely no sense at all. Let's say the organization represents LTV as a decimal number, where 0.82 represents an 82% LTV. In the data file, there will be a record with an LTV of 82.00. Using the business rule above, this would mean that the loan's LTV is 8200%. That is, of course, nonsense. Since you can't delete the record from the observation pool, you must decide what to do with it. You can leave it as is knowing that it will, most likely, skew your results and make them useless. You could *assume* that it is a data entry error and should be 0.82, not 82. But, what if that is not the case? What if it is supposed to be 8.20, or 820%? Maybe it should have been .0082, or 8.2%. This creates quite the dilemma for a Data Scientist, but he or she knows they can't eliminate the record because the total in the analysis will not match the institutions ledger.

One important question that your organization will need to grow comfortable answering is, what do you want to do with records with bad or missing data. Do you want to include the records and 'correct' the outlier data? Or, do you want to eliminate the record altogether? Does the entire record need to be eliminated from all analysis or only from analysis

155

that takes the bad or missing data into account? If the previous is true, then you will want to determine, as an organization, what the business rules for making corrections will be. For example, in the scenario above, my business rule could say that the LTV cannot be greater than 200%. Therefore, when I'm presented with a value of 8200%, I could just reset it to the maximum 200%. If the data is missing, I might plug-in an average value, arguing that it is more likely to be true that the LTV at origination of a loan was closer to the average than it was to 0%. These are the types of questions that you will need to ask during the integration and data modeling stage of your journey.

Data Velocity

Most data analytics and reporting are done using data snapshots, but data is gathered continuously in real-world operations at different velocities. Interest on accounts may be calculated once per month, not daily. Transactions on an account can happen at any time of the day. In reality, you don't want to try and conduct analysis on all of this data. Ideally, you want to be able to grab a significant point in time as a measurement. So how do you choose the best time to take a snapshot of a dataset? This is a question that becomes a big part of the requirements gathering and data modeling activity. For loan application process data, you may want to have daily snapshots so that you can measure turn-around time on application process steps. On portfolio loans, the snapshot may only need to be monthly because transactions on a loan account typically happen only once a month. Deposit accounts may require daily snapshots because you may want to measure account activity at various times in a day or days of the week.

But a certificate of deposit may only need monthly snapshots because, like loans, very little activity happens between the beginning and the end of the month. It is important to adjust your velocity for what you want to measure.

You also need to be cognizant of how different accounts behave, as it may inform what measurements you want to gather in your snapshot. For example, some credit card borrowers pay off their balances every month. If you take a snapshot of those accounts on a day where the balance has been paid, you don't get a realistic measurement of risk, because you did not capture what their balance was during the month. In this case, instead of capturing the account balance, it might be more informative to capture the average monthly balance which is often calculated on credit card accounts.

Once you have solved the problem of synchronizing internal data velocities, you may consider how you will integrate external data. For example, financial institutions may provide regulators with quarterly Call Reports. This information becomes public and you may want to integrate it with your internal data so that you can conduct benchmark analysis. If your account information is monthly and the external data is published quarterly, then you will want to decide how you want to synchronize it. For example, would you use a quarter-end snapshot or an average over time from your internal dataset? What if external data classifies loan and deposit data differently than you do internally? These are the types of questions you will want, and need, to answer as you consider how often you want to capture data for analysis.

Data Complexity

As mentioned previously, a single account with a single account owner is not particularly complex. When you start adding account owner and other account characteristics, then the problem becomes more complex. Take the simple example of a deposit account with two account owners. Some core systems will extract a separate, identical account record for each account owner when you run a query. The same is true for loans with multiple pieces of collateral. When this happens, you will, undoubtedly, get bad results. Take a look at the table below to see what I mean.

Account Owner	Acct #	Account Balance
Bob Smith	100123	$10,000.00
Sandra Smith	100123	$10,000.00
Barbara Martin	100124	$20,000.00

In many core data processing systems, if you try and pull data with account owner information joined with account information, then you may get something like you see above. You can see here that Bob and Sandra Smith are both owners of Account# 100123. Presumably, it is joint and they both have control over 100% of the money in the account. So, the entire account is associated with each individual, in effect, doubling the account balances for that one account in the table. If you were to total the Account Balances at this point, your result would be inflated by $10,000.

There are several ways to address this occurrence with business rules. There is no wrong answer, but there is exactly one bad answer, which is to leave this the way it is. One way you could handle this situation is to assign the balance to one account owner if you are able to extract only a 'primary' account owner. But you would clearly have to construct your extract to only select one of a multiple of account owners using a unique characteristic. This is depicted in Table A below. You could also distribute the total balance evenly among all account owners, as in Table B below. This method would require a little more finesse be added in the ETL process, but you may find it a more flexible method, especially when working with multiple pieces of collateral.

Table A

Account Owner	Acct #	Account Balance
Bob Smith	100123	$10,000.00
Barbara Martin	100124	$20,000.00

Table B

Account Owner	Acct #	Account Balance
Bob Smith	100123	$5,000.00
Sandra Smith	100123	$5,000.00
Barbara Martin	100124	$20,000.00

As you can see, both Table A and Table B provide the same total Account Balance when totaled, $30 thousand, but they are handled much differently. If you wanted to know the average deposit amount per account owner, Table B would be the best option. If you wanted to know the average deposit amount per account, the best scenario is Table A. The tables below illustrate a similar scenario, but with a twist using collateral instead of account owners.

Collateral	Acct #	Loan Balance
Collateral 1	100123	$10,000.00
Collateral 2	100123	$10,000.00
Collateral 3	100124	$20,000.00

Collateral	Acct #	Loan Balance
Collateral 1	100123	$10,000.00
Collateral 3	100124	$20,000.00

Collateral	Acct #	Loan Balance
Collateral 2	100123	$5,000.00
Collateral 2	100123	$5,000.00
Collateral 3	100124	$20,000.00

These are obviously simplistic examples of the type of complex scenarios you will encounter while defining how your data will be integrated and modeled. It is not the scope of this book to address all possible scenarios, or even the most common, but if you would like more information on working with data, you can visit the www.cubi.academy website for online tutorials.

Charge-Offs

Loan charge-offs create a unique challenge for many of the lenders I have worked with in the past. Specifically, their processes require that the loan type of a loan be changed when a loan is charged-off. For example, let's say the lender's loan type code for a new auto loan is 'NAL'. When the loan has not been charged-off, it is easy to use the loan type as a dimension and categorize loans by their loan type. But, when a loan is charged off, however, the core data processor may require the lender to change the loan type code to CHDOFF to signify that the loan is charged off, and presumably, to identify that this loan should no longer be included in the open loan balances. What this does, however, is eliminate the ability of the lender to do any analysis on loans charged off by loan type. Obviously, this does not make a lot of sense, but it is the reality for many lenders. Lenders who use this process should consider how they want to accommodate this going forward when integrating and modeling their data.

Ideally, there would be a way to preserve the original loan type in the organization's data repository, if not in the core data processor itself. I bring this up in this section as it is certainly something that should be considered in the integration and modeling strategy. As data is extracted from the core data processing system, a process to translate collateral types or purposes codes, identifying the loan type, might be required to accurately define the original loan type of the loan if the loan type has already been changed. Whatever strategy is used, however, the idea of simply transferring the current loan type that references a charge-off should be rejected. It will make your data utterly useless.

Another issue that arises specifically with charged off loans is how to keep track of charge-off amounts in the data repository. Once a loan is charged-off, a charge-off amount is typically recorded in a charge-off field. A charge-off date is also recorded. Some core systems, however, leave the outstanding balance in the loan balance field. In the data repository, you would want the loan balance to be set to zero or the net remaining balance, if the charge-off was not 100% of the loan balance, so that metrics built on the Loan Balance fields would not be skewed. In addition, it is often the case that charge-off amounts are updated as recoveries occur, or additional costs are applied. Because of the way snapshots are extracted from the core, the charge-off amounts may not be cumulative, but may only be for the most current transaction amount. Transferring this data to the data repository without considering how to calculate a running balance might also skew charge-off totals.

Software-as-a-Service(Saas)

There are many vendors out there who offer SaaS which support the quick and efficient deployment of data analytics. Many of these solutions offer data warehousing capabilities, at least in a limited form. They will consume your data files and store it in a format that makes it easy to deploy the common metrics that financial institutions need for decision-making. These offerings can considerably reduce the amount of time that it takes to transform your business to a data-driven culture. However, there are some things you should consider when opting for this choice.

Typically, these solutions focus on one area of the financial institutions business, such as Marketing or Lending. As such, their embedded metrics are not always useful to the enterprise, only to a single department. For example, a loan portfolio analytics solution may not take householder information into account like a marketing analytics solution may. You may find this restrictive and want to choose a more enterprise friendly approach.

Often, to appeal to the needs of the masses, a purpose for which SaaS solutions are ideal, the provider asks you to conform to their business rules versus the software conforming to your organization's rules. This is problematic when you have special circumstances such as commercial or student loans, or loan participations. If the software wasn't designed to support these unique circumstances, you will find yourself only being able to use it for a fraction of your analysis and grappling to conduct analysis on the other loans in an Excel® spreadsheet.

Finally, as mentioned above, because of the limited scope of these offerings, they do not consume all your data. Therefore, you will find that you are still required to create a repository for data to house all the other data you want to analyze. In fact, I would recommend, regardless of what you use to visualize your business intelligence, you should think about a data repository that is designed to support your financial institution's needs, first. Then if you decide to integrate a SaaS solution into your analytics process, it makes it much easier when you can simply transfer data from your repository to the providers data warehouse.

Data Security and the Cloud

Data integration and modeling for business intelligence is much different than archiving data for recovery or backup reasons. All too often, financial institutions are tempted to integrate and model ALL their data in a central repository and then, for security reasons, lock it down so that only certain people, with the proper authority, can access it. First, you should know that this violates the core theory of data warehousing and business intelligence. In fact, the whole purpose for the movement to create data warehouses and pursue enterprise business intelligence solutions was to create an environment where anyone any the organization could access business data and answer business questions on their own. Other than for security software applications, there should be no real need to include private customer information into your business intelligence data warehouse. It is not intended to be an Customer Relationship Management solution. The environment should be used for Business Intelligence and Data Analytics, not managing individual accounts.

For the reasons stated above, there is really no reason why a data repository built for business intelligence and data analytics could not be deployed to the cloud. You may ask, "what if I want to extract a list of prospects for certain product-based offers upon concluding some segmentation analysis?" That is a great question and is easily answered. Your cloud data repository should have a unique identifier for each individual and account that, when downloaded, could be cross-referenced with an internal database to extract confidential information about that person or account. Even if your organization wants to build an on-premise data warehouse for all its data, data marts, as described previously, can be deployed to the cloud for business intelligence and data analytics that do not include confidential information. The problem with on-premise deployments is that they can make access extremely restrictive and hamper integration with other cloud services. Having a data warehouse or data mart in the cloud provides easy access and flexibility that on-premise facilities have difficulty matching.

The data integration and modeling process is one of the critical pieces of the puzzle when transforming to a data-driven decision culture. A considerable amount of time will be consumed considering all the scenarios you may encounter when accessing data for decision-making, but it is important not to fall into the temptation of short-cutting the process. You will end up severely restricting your capabilities in the future. It may be necessary to seek the assistance of data consultants to assist your organization during this stage of the process as these consultants have a great deal more experience working through these issues with other financial institutions like yours.

Chapter 9

Analytics: Descriptive, Predictive and Prescriptive

A data-driven decision culture requires that the data used for decision-making is accurately informing business decisions. However, making that the case in your organization may be a complicated endeavor. You may find that data that you have access to for decision-making is of little use or, if it is used, provides disappointing results that fall short of what you need. Ronald H. Coase[31] was said to have remarked, "If you torture data enough, it will confess to anything." His sentiment was that one can make data support any pre-conceived opinion or business decision, whether it be right or wrong. Using data to reinforce bias is not what decision-makers in a data-driven decision culture do. Instead, data-driven cultures are allowing data analytics to guide them into new opportunities and ways of thinking. To this end, there are three segmentations of data analytics that make up a well-structured data-driven culture: descriptive analytics which tell the story of what has happened; predictive analytics which tell the

---

[31] https://en.wikiquote.org/wiki/Ronald_Coase

story of what could happen; and prescriptive analytics which helps us determine what needs to be done when something happens. In this chapter I will present an explanation of all three.

Descriptive Analytics

Descriptive Analytics, as one might assume, is using data to describe and explain events that have already happened. We see descriptive facts in every facet of our lives, from rating a quarterback in the NFL to viewing usage statistics on our mobile device. We literally measure almost everything we do or that is done in the world around us and we like to attempt to interpret meaning from those measurements. However, we do not always extract the right meaning from those measurements, or facts. In fact, our interpretations of facts are sometimes exactly opposite of their meaning.

For example, after the 2018 mid-term elections, many media outlets reported that voter turn-out was a record high between 48% and 49%[32]. But, there was nothing statistically significant about the 2018 mid-term elections in comparison to all mid-term elections in U.S. history. In fact, the average voter turnout rate of mid-term elections in the U.S., since the late 1700's, is about 49%. While the *Fortune* online article cited above is technically correct that the 2018 turnout was the highest since 1914, it fails to mention that the turn-out rate was about the same in 1966 as it was in 2018. To this point, if every mid-term election since 1914 had the same

---

[32] http://fortune.com/2018/11/14/voter-turnout-highest-level-since-1914/

49% turnout, then it could be said of each of them that they were the highest since 1914. That is not informative.

The highest voter turnout ever, for a mid-term election was 71.4%, and the lowest turnout was 21.6%[33]. In other words, voter turnout tends to ebb and flow over time. Voter turn-out in 2018 was not unprecedented[34], as reported by the media, even though it was highest among more recent years. In fact, it was only in the 55th percentile of all mid-term elections statistics. The point here is that news reporters read the descriptive data related to voter turnout, or more likely repeated an interpretation in a press release, and instead of finding that it was about average over all time, concluded that it was significantly high and worthy of being reported as historic.

What's interesting is that either political party could be guilty of over-stating the significance of voter turnout in 2018. For sure, the races for a number of offices were pivotal and very close. Each side could point to turnout and claim that the turnout is somehow indicative of the level of concern voters have over each party's political agenda or to congratulate themselves for their grass roots efforts. That is the interesting thing about descriptive analytics, it can often be interpreted in several ways if it is interpreted without also including some contextual data for perspective.

For example, voter participation in the United Kingdom and Canada has also been on the rise since the year 2000[35]. I'm not sure that the cause

---

[33] http://www.electproject.org/national-1789-present

[34] https://fivethirtyeight.com/features/the-2018-midterms-in-4-charts/

and effect has been established to date as political parties would rather explain voting trends in a way that is favorable to their agenda than determine if there is another significant societal factor. I suspect there is something driving this trend, and while each party in the U.S. would have you believe that it is their agenda that is driving voter participation, the fact is that party agendas haven't change all that much in the past 50 years and certainly cannot explain the trends that are also observed in Canada and the U.K. One might be tempted to say that the information age and social media is driving a rise in participation rates because one could point to a correlation to social media activity and voter participation over the past decade, but that doesn't explain why voter participation, at its current high, is 30% lower than it was all throughout the 1800's. It would appear that there are other human behavioral factors at work and that voter participation is not just on the rise in the U.S. but also in other similarly situated countries. As an aside, voter participation is declining globally, so the voting trends in the U.S., U.K., and Canada contradict global trends.

Of course, I digress as this is not intended to be a book on political reporting or national elections, but I thought my example above would be slightly more interesting than discussing the statistical significance of a 25 basis-points change in deposit activity at a financial institution. It serves my purpose in demonstrating that descriptive analytics goes beyond simply reporting facts. More importantly, descriptive analytics, if properly executed, will tell you what facts mean in context with the world around you. You will often read in the trade press that loan delinquency is

---

[35] https://www.idea.int/data-tools/data/voter-turnout

falling as loan growth climbs. Well, of course, this is exactly what should happen; it is not news. But, these articles often have a tone that suggests that the world is a better place and that we should all be happy. They insinuate that while more people are borrowing, which is a sign of growth, credit quality is better because delinquency is down. The truth is that loan delinquency will always go down, in the short-term, as loan growth rises, because the denominator in the loan delinquency equation is growing larger as the numerator remains constant. Newer loans do not default at the same rate as older, more mature, loans. Reporting statistics out of context is not an example of descriptive analytics. Descriptive analytics attempts to determine and explain why a statistic is relevant.

Two decades ago, U.S. credit unions did not participate in indirect auto lending in high numbers. The leadership of most credit unions felt that indirect auto loans carried more inherent risk than direct auto loans and the idea of participating in a business relationship with auto dealers went against their long-held values of protecting their members. Over the years, however, credit unions found that it was increasing more difficult to compete with large banks with a national presence without at least attempting to capture auto loans at the point of sale. Many credit unions began to reconsider their philosophies and began putting their financial toes into the "shark-infested" waters of point-of-sale auto lending. The trouble is, many of their employees, who had long been indoctrinated to distrust auto dealers, didn't necessarily embrace these new third-party relationships. This resulted in some interesting developments.

About thirteen years ago, I was working with a credit union client in my area who called me, panicked, saying that examiners had shut-down their indirect auto lending program because the examiners had identified a sharp increase in Indirect delinquencies and the credit union had no strategy to rectify the situation. I was puzzled that the credit union had such a dramatic increase in indirect auto loan delinquency that had gone unrecognized in their reporting. What my investigation uncovered was alarming; the credit union was not reporting on indirect auto loans separately from direct auto loans. Therefore, there was no way for them to know what was happening in that specialized portfolio. Significant to the credit union at that point in time was the fact that their entire next year's strategy was dependent on their indirect auto lending program which was then placed on an indefinite hiatus by examiners.

While the lack of reporting was a significant discovery, I was still puzzled that indirect auto loans were significantly more delinquent than direct auto loans. There is, typically, some differences in performance between direct and indirect auto loans, but the differences are not typically significant or, as in this case, catastrophic. I agreed to investigate their program and report back with my findings. Long story short, what I found out was even more shocking than the lack of reporting and the delinquency itself. I discovered that the individual in charge of collections in the credit union was part of the old guard that did not support the credit union's participation in indirect auto lending. Her strategy, in defiance of the credit unions paradigm shift, was to simply ignore indirect loans as they became delinquent. Indirect members didn't get calls or notices when their accounts went delinquent and these loans tended to default and charge-off at a higher rate due to a lack of attention.

It would have been easy to simply look at the statistics and assume that, on the surface, indirect auto loans present a significantly higher risk than direct auto loans, solely based upon where the loan originated. However, the credit union's indirect auto loan experience didn't match that of other, similar-sized, credit unions in the same region. Therefore, it was important to dig deeper into the issue to discover the exact cause of the anomaly. This step is often skipped when making business decisions and, as a result, businesses often restrict their opportunities by reacting only to statistics without conducting the analysis. For example, when lenders see accounts not performing as expected, based on descriptive data, they tend to stop offering those products altogether instead of also analyzing what is working within that same line of business to see if there are opportunities for improving performance overall.

Interestingly, almost the exact same scenario as above occurred at another credit union a decade later. The CEO began complaining of higher than average losses in the credit union indirect auto lending portfolio. While the CEO was tempted to simply blame the issue on the specific type of business and abandon the program, he called on me in to investigate the problem. As I looked through all the credit union's portfolio data, I could find no significant differences between the underwriting practices of indirect auto loan underwriters and direct auto loan underwriters. In fact, they were the same people. Anecdotally, however, I began to hear that, internally, there were divisions among the lending staff about the value of indirect auto lending and there was a strong lobby among the staff to eliminate indirect auto lending in favor of direct auto lending strategies. This made me suspicious that the same thing that had happened a decade earlier was now happening again in another credit union. So, I began asking for portfolio management data, instead of simply looking at underwriting and program management data. Suddenly, my contacts at the credit union were non-responsive and there was no longer a desire to dig into that issue any further. When business leaders look only at statistics and do not insist on proper analytics, not only are mistakes made in decision-making, but bad behavior can go undetected for far too long.

Predictive Analytics

Often, Predictive Analytics intimidate decision-makers. As the term insinuates, predictive analytics is about predicting behavior based on historic facts. Pontificating on future events has been the exclusive domain of decision-makers for decades and predictive analytics suggests that the skill and domain of those decision-makers is no longer required. Lisa Burrell, Editorial Director at the MIT Sloan Management Review, comments on this sentiment in its 2019 Winter installment[36]. There is also a fear that predictive analytics, especially among member-centric credit union leaders, fails to treat members like individuals. Putting members in a statistical box is difficult for many of my clients.

---

[36] https://sloanreview.mit.edu/article/artificial-intelligence-brings-out-the-worst-and-the-best-in-us/

For example, I have worked with dozens of credit unions to help them improve their automated credit decision rules. Typically, I find that there are a statistically significant number of credit applications that are approved, typically very high credit score borrowers, no matter the circumstances. I would call these applications 'no-brainers' as they require little work from loan underwriters. On the other hand, I also find a significantly high number of applicants who are never approved for a loan, like 95%, when a decision rule is broken. Oddly, my clients have been willing to adopt recommended changes to improve the system approval rate of high credit score borrowers but are very resistant to auto-declining the applicants that are manually declined 95% of the time. That means that only one out of twenty borrowers with the identified characteristic would be approved. These credit unions want to give even the worst borrowers every opportunity to be approved for a loan, even if it means giving them a loan in error because a significant factor gets missed in the manual underwriting process. An old mentor of mine once told me that nearly every loan loss he has seen has been due to an underwriter overlooking a critical detail on a credit application. I'm not sure that is true, but statistics and trends mean things and you shouldn't ignore the facts.

We use predictive analytics every day of our lives when we use our intuition to make decisions in areas where we have a lot of experience. We can predict accurately, for example, that traffic will be heavy on the way to work in the morning. We can predict that we are not going to be our best in the evening as we come to the close of our day. These predictions are made based on our experience of historic events.

I used to spend a lot of time with my granddad who owned a plumbing company when I was a teenager. Every time he arrived on a service call, he would grab his steel toolbox and sponge, then head to the door of the residence. If I asked you to list tools used by a plumber, it is likely that you would not list a sponge. But, my granddads experience taught him that there was a high probability that, in addition to his other tools, he would need a sponge while working with water. He wasn't a wizard, or smarter than the rest of us, he just allowed his experience to inform him.

There are some predictions, however, that do not come as easily, especially those related to rare events or those we do not observe due to cognitive bias. For this reason, we need predictive analytics to inform our decisions. I've seen some interesting, previously unknown, trends that popup a lot when I work on predictive models for financial institutions. One that I typically get considerable pushback on is that co-borrowers on loans have a significant impact on loan performance. In fact, the impact is so great that it should affect pricing. I have seen that co-borrowers can reduce the probability of default by as much as 66%. In other words, a borrower by themselves is 300% more likely to default on a loan than if you pair that borrower with someone else. Now, a lot of lenders will tell you that a high percentage of co-borrowers on defaulted loans will not pay the deficiency balance. This can also be true, which means those co-borrowers were probably not that good, which is why the loan defaulted in the first place. But, if you look inside the portfolio of performing loans, co-borrowers are impacting timely payments more than one can readily visualize based solely on default patterns. The problem is, we tend to only analyze the bad, not the good.

Another interesting characteristic I have found in many lender portfolios is that longer term loans neither necessarily have a higher default rate than shorter term loans, nor do they necessarily have a substantially longer average life. What I have found is that longer term loans, with terms greater than 72 months, often have a lower default rate than loans with terms between 60 and 72 months; however, the longer-term loans tend to default earlier in the loan pool lifecycle. This tells a bit of a story that is important for loan pricing and loss predictions. With a lower default rate, one is tempted to say that a lower risk premium should be applied to the loan and thus result in a slightly lower rate. Yet, because when the loans that do default do so earlier in their lifecycle, the loss severity will likely be higher than shorter term loans, perhaps offsetting gains due to fewer defaults. These two facts, interact with one another, so it would be difficult to make decisions on risk based on one of these facts independently, although that is what often happens. It is wise to analyze how statistics interact with each other before developing a conclusion.

Recently accounting guideline changes, related to reserving for losses, require businesses, especially financial institutions, to develop default and loss probabilities, or predictions. While this is not the only application of predictive analytics for a credit union, it has quickly become one of the most important and complex. The reason that it has become so important is that it is required, while most analytics projects are discretionary. It is complex because it involves more than a single predictive model. Current Expected Credit Losses (CECL) requires a predictive default and loss model, a predictive loan life model, a predictive cost of funds model and a model to predict the impact of external economic factors that might put stress on a loan portfolio's performance. For a data geek, like myself, I could not have dreamt of a better time to be in the Data Science business. However, I can see how this scenario can be quite disruptive and frustrating for a financial institution, especially when there are far more interesting things to try and predict. But, what if the exercise of creating these mandatory models paved the way for your credit union to become a better lender. With the level of intelligence gained by conducting the analysis required to build these CECL models, lenders can now discover new opportunities for making loans and increasing their competitive edge.

This is what inspired me to create The RiskGenie™, software which allows lenders to embed these predictive models into the lending process rather than simply using them to calculate allowance for loan losses after the fact. When these models are embedded into the lending process, they can be used in both the automated lending environment to provide dynamic pricing for loans rather than categorical pricing which is used today, and they could enable underwriters to tailor loan offers to meet the need of individual borrowers. Instead of treating everyone the same, each member is treated as an individual. So predictive analytics could serve to individualize service rather than boxing members in.

Predictive models can obviously be used for purposes other than lending and some financial institutions have already started down the path of predicting member behavior. As a consumer of financial services, I'd much rather that the direct offers I get from my financial institution be tailored for my needs, based on the information I provide my financial institution in the transactions that I execute with them and, perhaps, information that I make publicly available. For example, I'm an automotive enthusiast, so I like the latest and greatest in transportation offerings. Admittedly, for this reason, I don't keep cars or trucks very long before I'm looking for a fresh set of wheels. I've had my driver's license for thirty-five years and I have had twenty-two vehicles registered in my name. Each time I decide to purchase a new car, I must do exactly the same thing. I do my vehicle research and then I go to the dealer to make my purchase. I fill out a credit application at the dealership and finance my vehicle with the dealer's finance company and take all the rebates I can get. About a month later, I get a letter or postcard from my credit union offering to refinance my vehicle at a super low rate and to give me a $100 gift card. I call the credit union where I'm asked to complete another credit application and then refinance my vehicle at a lower rate. It is the same process every time and I always get approved. Now, it seems to me that a little predictive modeling might serve both me and my financial institution a little better.

If I were to build a predictive model for the above scenario, I might monitor borrowers' loan repayment habits and try to predict when they were going to make another auto purchase or trade. I would then work with a network of dealers to create offers tailored specifically for my member based upon their ability to pay, driving habits and vehicle preferences. I would also ensure that any special pricing or incentives offered were based upon the member financing their vehicle purchase with my financial institution. You may ask yourself, why would you do all that, if you could just offer to refinance a vehicle purchase after the fact. My question, in response, would be, what is the pull-through rate on those recapture offers?

Quicken Loans has figured out the value of keeping a customer and they have determined that the cost of keeping their customers happy with their mortgage loan is less than the cost of attempting to recapture a loan after their customer has gone elsewhere. Unlike my other financial institutions, Quicken Loans, who holds my mortgage, will contact me every couple of years and offer to refinance my house at a lower rate if available and waive most, if not all, the closing costs. Why would they do that? Well, retaining a loan customer is cheaper than acquiring a new one. They are predicting that, under certain conditions, I may begin to look at opportunities to refinance my loan myself. They want to head me off at the pass and they know that when people refinance their homes they take cash out, raising the loan balance and extending the term. They are simply mining the customers they already have, and they are basing their offers on information they have gathered from publicly available sources. They are tailoring their offers to those that best fit their customer's needs.

Is a predictive model right all the time? If it is built correctly, it is. That doesn't mean that it predicts, with 100% accuracy, which customer will behave absolutely one way or the other. Every predictive model is based on probability and has variance. It is probable that not all borrowers with a 500-credit-score will default and not repay their loan, but it is highly probable that most will. It is also probable that at least a few 800-credit-score borrowers will default on a loan, but most will not. The question is, does the model fit the real world? Predictive modeling isn't about getting it right 100% of the time, it's about optimizing the use of your resources for the best possible outcome for you and your members. As I said earlier, you can predict that traffic will be heavy during rush hour but that doesn't mean that traffic won't be heavy at any other time of the day. But, if you want to get somewhere spending the least amount of time in traffic, you are more likely to do so by waiting until after rush hour.

Please allow me one more example from the real world of predictive analytics. Walmart is one of the world's largest retailers, but I remember a time in my life when they weren't. Like your credit union, they started small and grew to their current size by attracting satisfied customers. They are sometimes criticized and the subject of jokes, but they are able to walk the tight rope of efficient retail operations while maintaining a customer satisfaction level that sustains growth and profitability. Do they make everyone happy? No. Is everyone wowed by their experience shopping at Walmart? No. Can you get exactly the brand of toothpaste you want at the lowest price at Walmart? Yes. They are not trying to be Neiman Marcus. They have measured the risks and made strategic decisions that allow them to remain the low-cost leader they set out to be.

Despite the very basic trappings of Walmart, your engagement with the company is highly engineered, perhaps more than with any other retailer[37].

They analyze everything and have models in place to optimize operations to keep costs low. For example, you have probably noticed that not every checkout register at Walmart is manned by a cashier all the time. In fact, while they have, at least, a couple of dozen checkout lanes in any given store, it seems that no more than two live cashiers are working the registers at any given time. Except that isn't true. The number of checkout lanes that are present in every store represent the number needed at peak traffic hours, but the number of cashiers is based on current traffic. You probably don't always go at peak hours. In fact, you probably optimize your time by going to Walmart at hours you predict there will be fewer people there. If you go to Walmart at five o'clock in the morning, there is a good chance that your only option will be self-checkout (Don't ask me how I know that). Even though the existence of only two or three cashiers seems outrageous when there are so many checkout lanes that could be open, I would be willing to bet that you have not waited behind more than one other person in line at any given time. It just seems intolerable because we can see the other checkout lanes not being used. If you go to Walgreen's, on the other hand, you don't get as upset if you have to wait in line, because there is only one or two registers. Walmart is using predictive analytics to optimize its resources to keep their costs low while providing a high enough level of service to you to keep you coming back.

---

[37] https://www.dezyre.com/article/how-big-data-analysis-helped-increase-walmarts-sales-turnover/109

About Walmart, I was curious what their most popular items were. Since they do so much analysis, I was sure that I could find the information somewhere. They publish a state by state list of their most popular items[38]. In Texas, where I live, the most popular item is TV Wall Mounts. Go figure. In California it is Protein Drink Mix and in D.C. its Great Value French Fried Onions! While their number one selling item nationally, bananas[39], doesn't show up as any single state's number one item, do you know where they do show up? Near the register where you are waiting in line, that's where. This information doesn't really have anything to do with predictive analytics, but I did think it was interesting and thought I would pass it along.

Prescriptive Analytics

There hasn't been much talk about prescriptive analytics to date, but it represents the future state of data-driven decision-making. It is the answer to the question, what do I do with that information? Prescriptive analytics is the discipline of modeling the best remedy to a given problem revealed through data analytics. Prescriptive analytics are the ultimate step in the analytics process as it, obviously, suggests what should happen as result of the first two analytical steps. Beyond simply predicting what will happen, prescriptive analytics offer the best next step to solving the problem.

---

[38] https://sc.cnbcfm.com/applications/cnbc.com/resources/files/2018/01/09/walmart.com-Top-Sellers-of-2017.jpg

[39] https://www.theblaze.com/news/2015/06/04/walmarts-no-1-selling-item-isnt-at-all-what-youd-expect

A lot of data analytics is being built into our automobiles today to provide more safety and a better driving experience. When I learned to drive, we used a lot of descriptive analytics, but they were not built into my '75 Plymouth Valiant. We would survey the roadway and maneuver to avoid accidents. If we ended up in a ditch, we could say, with great certainty, we made a driving error and lost control of our vehicle. We didn't really predict what would happen when we drove too fast for conditions and we, obviously, didn't have access to prescriptive analytics to inform us how to best stay out of trouble. My car today, built in 2015, has an indicator that tells me when it is probable that the roadway is freezing. A polite tone is emitted, and a visual aid informs me that the temperature has dropped to a certain point. That is descriptive. My wife's car, built in 2017 has lane departure warning which alerts her when the vehicle is leaving the lane she is traveling in. This is predictive because it is taking in the descriptive data and predicting, based on that information, that the vehicle will leave the lane of travel if corrective action is not taken. However, the system doesn't offer any feedback as to what to do. Recently, I rented a car built in 2018. Not only did it have lane departure warning technology, but it had prescriptive capabilities in that it would adjust the steering wheel to stay in the lane, instead of allowing me to veer off the road. Before I realized how the feature was working, I thought I had a flat tire because the vehicle seemed to steer itself but was happy when I discovered that the car was trying to save my life. I had never had that level of relationship with my automobile.

Ideally, you want to get to the same place in your business where automobiles are today. You want to have a symbiotic relationship with your members. You don't want to take away the entire joy and satisfaction of running the credit union by supplanting decision-makers with computers, but it is certainly nice to have a computer there helping to nudge you in the right direction. What if you had facial recognition technology embedded in your branch security cameras and you could recognize your member as they walked through the door (Descriptive)? Then the cameras transferred the member data to your core data processing system and looked up the member's account before they approached the service counter. The facial recognition technology could also try and interpret their mood based upon facial expressions (Predictive). When the member approached the counter, their account information is already displayed on the service representative's computer. The representative is given a suggested greeting based on the member's mood, and product offerings are provided based on the member's account data (Prescriptive). Your teller never asked for identification, the member doesn't have to fumble around for their account number, and because your systems sensed frustration, your teller is prepared to ease the member's concerns.

Would the scenario above benefit your organization? Would it benefit your member? Does the technology exist to support this scenario? The answer to all these questions is yes. The only thing that, perhaps, keeps you from deploying this scenario in your organization is a data-driven decision culture.

Chapter 10

Data Visualization

Twenty-five years ago, when I served on the local school board, I had the opportunity to attend an educational conference where the primary subject was regional demographics. As I made my way to the back corner of the conference room for one of the breakout sessions, I noticed an overhead projector set up in the middle of the room. The presenter entered the room just as the time came to start the session, closed the door behind him, made his way to the projector and flipped a switch to turn it on. As the projector began to hum to life, the presenter pulled out a transparency slide and placed it on the stage glass and the slide's content was displayed on the whiteboard at the front of the room. As the presenter began his presentation with a slow, quiet voice that you could barely hear, he read, line for line, the spreadsheet of numbers on the screen that now covered the entire wall in the front of the room. In that very moment, I realized that I was stuck with nowhere to go. I couldn't just get up and walk out of the room without disrupting the presenter, so I sat in misery for the remainder of the forty-five-minute session. I learned two things that day;

One, never sit in the back of the room with no clear exit to the door, and two, presentation of data should be interesting to the audience, not just the to the presenter.

Data visualization is the presentation of data for analysis and decision-making. It can take on many forms. Technically speaking, the overhead projection of a demographic spreadsheet is a form of data visualization, albeit an ineffective one in my experience. As data visualization has progressed, there has been a lot of focus placed on 'dashboards', which I will discuss later, in place of printed reports but it is important to understand that, while they provide a high level of flexibility, dashboards are not the only way to visualize data. As I work with organizations on data transformation projects, I always ask stakeholders how they prefer to consume business intelligence and have found that there is still a warm place in many a heart for the basic printed report. The three most important things to remember when it comes to data visualization, above the presentation method, is that it is accurate, it is accessible and that it is actionable by the decision-maker, or stakeholder. The visualization method is secondary to these priorities.

I had the opportunity to work with a software product team, in the past, which produced a loan portfolio analytics tool for financial institutions. At the time, the technology was truly state of the art in that it employed a sophisticated data cube which provided quick access to very large datasets, reducing the amount of time required for analytics within a credit union. In the early days, the product provided a high level of accuracy, as long as the input data was accurate to begin with. But, most importantly, anybody in the organization could access the data via an online presentation layer with formatted charts, graphs, and data grids. There was only one problem, we soon figured out. Our clients didn't want online dashboards, they wanted reports that they could print and distribute because that is the way the organization consumed business intelligence. We could have insisted that our clients 'get with it', but instead, we wisely decided to embed the ability to not only print reports, but to schedule reports for distribution in our second iteration of the product. It is great to be innovative and trendy, but if in doing so, your initiative becomes disruptive to the organization, it is truly time wasted in the end.

You have probably noticed that your automobile dashboard is able to provide you with considerably more information than it could in the past. Of course, when I started to drive, there were only a couple of instruments in the dash that were of utmost importance, the speedometer, and the gas gauge. If I had a manual transmission, I would have probably also had a tachometer that measured RPM's. Today, I can check the oil level in my car, I can measure my average fuel efficiency, and I can check the air pressure in my tires without leaving the confines and protection of the driver's compartment. While I can read all these measurements from a single dashboard, they are not all available at the same time. What hasn't changed, however, is that the speedometer, fuel gauge and tachometer are still front and center on most, if not all vehicle dashboards. Imagine what would happen if automakers removed, or hid, those standard instruments as vehicles become smarter and do more things for us. Auto buyers will be resistant to that change. Newer technologies provide more flexibility than the past and provide more extensive information, but the need for basic performance information hasn't changed and automakers have respected those sensitivities among their customers.

As you lead the transformation of your organization to one that makes data-driven decisions, you must respect the sensitivities of your stakeholders. With confusion comes distrust and when your stakeholders distrust the data provided to them, it becomes useless in decision-making. Therefore, before I present information about the various visualization tools available for data analytics, let me review the importance of data accuracy, accessibility and actionability in more detail.

Data Accuracy

The accuracy of the data presented in your visualizations is not just about whether things add up, it is about whether the data tells the story that it is intended to communicate. Let's begin with the underlying raw data that support the metrics in your visualization. The consumer of data, the business stakeholder, must understand what the data is presenting. Referring to my story in the first paragraph, it was clear the overhead slide was presenting demographic data, a lot of demographic data. The data was broken down by zip code in the region each attendees' school districts was located. For each zip code there were metrics broken down for each race category, measuring current population and projected growth. There was a lot of detail and the data was, potentially, informative. However, it wasn't easy to discern anything of relevance because the large amount of data wasn't grouped in a way that made it readily informative to me. The zip codes in a single school district were not necessarily incremental, but the zip codes in the presenter's slide were listed in numeric order, which means that each line of data would bounce back and forth from one school district to another as one would read through the slide. There was no grouping of zip codes that promised the greatest shift in demographics over time, so there was no particular story to tell. What if a zip code was missing that should have be included for my district? I would not have been able to readily identify any missing data the way it was being presented in the slide. The presenter, in this case, did not take his audience into account and simply presented that data as it seemed relevant to him. It is incumbent upon the person who prepares the data presentation to ensure that the data is telling the story the consumer wants told and to disclose any potential problems with the underlying data that may exist.

It is equally important to consider data's perceived accuracy if data has been filtered out of a report or dashboard. The two charts below appear to display the same data. The title of the two charts is the same and the segmentation of the data is the same. However, it is easy to see that the proportions are somewhat different, with the black population making up a larger proportion in chart two than in chart one. To the casual viewer, it would be difficult to question either one of these charts presented in isolation. Meaning, if you only showed me one of the charts, I wouldn't be able to discern any inaccuracies in the data. But the trouble is, a decision-maker may draw the wrong conclusion because they do not know the context of the data. Therefore, it is important for the presenter of the data to provide details about the context.

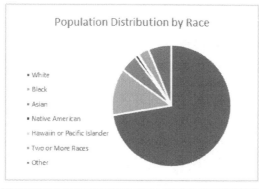

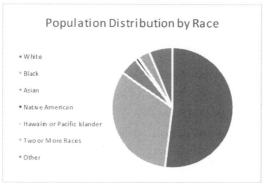

In the case above, if data is eliminated from the visualization for some reason, it should be indicated in the presentation itself. If chart one is representative of all, unfiltered, data, then there should be a notation of such just below. For example, the notation could state, "All unfiltered population data from 2009 voluntary census survey." If chart two represents corrections, filters, or differences in collection methods, it could be notated like this, "Corrected data from compulsory census registration, 2009." In my opinion, it is ethically questionable, in data science, to use data to skew conclusions by not providing details about where the data comes from. But even if you do not believe it to be a question of ethics, you will want to consider the impact on credibility if, under scrutiny, the validity of your data comes into question.

Besides accuracy in the data source itself, you must ensure that the metrics used in visualizations are calculated correctly and their meaning is clear. Misunderstandings can arise when either the metric is not calculated correctly, or its meaning is intentionally vague. I've seen at least a couple of instances of this in my work with clients. In one case, a data analyst prepared a report that purportedly compared market share between the company and its competitors on a national basis. As I began to ask questions about the data, I found that the analyst was only using data from the markets the company was operating in to measure the company's share of the market but was using national statistics to measure its competitors. The result made it appear as if the competitor was not doing as well as the company because their sales were divided among a much larger denominator (national sales) versus the company's sales being divided by a smaller denominator (regional sales). This is not just an error in science, it is an egregious ethical error, as it provided an extremely skewed vision of reality for decision-makers. The second instance I recall was when I was working with a lending client who was incorrectly reporting loan delinquency. Delinquency measurements are made by dividing the total amount of delinquent loans by the total amount of all loans. If you segment the portfolio into loan types, the calculation is principally the same, the total delinquent loans of that loan type, divided by all loans of that same loan type. What this lender was doing, however, was dividing the delinquent loans of a loan type by all loans in the entire portfolio. This resulted in segmented delinquency measurements being extremely lower than they were. I don't need to point out the problems that this type of error can create and I'm not quite sure if the client was unaware of how to correctly calculate delinquency or if the they were calculating delinquency incorrectly on purpose.

While it is tempting to only present data that is favorable to your position, this violates all principles of data science. Data science is about studying data to make better decisions. If the presentation of data is designed to support a position and not a decision, then it is not being used properly. One may not care about this distinction but if you violate this principle, it will not be long before data in your organization is not trusted and all the effort and investment contributed to a data infrastructure will be lost. People simply won't trust that data. To be honest, I've seen more organizations misuse and abuse data than I have witnessed organizations use data to guide decision-making at this point. It really is disappointing and one of the primary reasons I recommend organizations appoint one person to be responsible for data analytics and business intelligence. It doesn't matter whether you refer to that person as the Chief Data Officer or the lead data analyst, there needs to be one person who understands data science in your organization and who is ultimately responsible for the data's veracity.

Data Accessibility

Admittedly, it is somewhat odd to discuss data accessibility in an age when data security is such a prevalent issue. I suspect that many organizations, and especially financial institutions, have serious concerns about making data available for just anyone in the organization to consume. Unfortunately, the effect of these concerns has been delays in data projects that last months or years, and failures to achieve the highest potential of what business intelligence can accomplish in an organization. But, accessibility goes well beyond just data security.

Let's begin by taking data security off the table. Besides security and fraud analytics, sensitive data is not required for most business intelligence projects. You don't need an account owners name and address to calculate delinquency, for example. To this end, the organization should split data into two segments. While a central data warehouse or data lake can house both sensitive and non-sensitive data together, the organization should segment data containing confidential or sensitive information into one data mart and non-sensitive data into another data mart for everyday data analysis. What happens, however, as organizations start down the path of data transformation, is they begin by thinking in terms of single solutions, like building a single data warehouse or repository. However, part of the organization's strategy should be to define how data can be organized to ensure that sensitive data is protected, and non-sensitive data can be made accessible. What I've seen is organizations attempting to head down the transformation path while retaining the old I.T. gatekeeper paradigm, which creates a bottleneck in the data stream.

For organization decision-makers, there should be a central data repository that they can access individually with one of the tools described later in this chapter. They should not have to request data or report projects from your I.T. team. With access to a data warehouse designed for business intelligence activities, they have ready-made metrics and dimensions at their disposal. They do not have recreate the wheel every time they do an analysis. If they choose to, or feel the need to, they can dive deeper into raw data for experimentation and perhaps recommend new informative metrics or dimensions. If data is restricted or held back, what typically happens is that decision-makers choose not to include data in their decision making rather than wait for data to be delivered to them.

Data Actionability

Actionable data tells a story. When presenting data, whether it be a formatted report or dashboard, the presentation should help the decision-maker draw a conclusion. Too often, there is a temptation to overload reports and dashboards with useless information based on the belief that more data establishes credibility. However, in a well-formed data environment, the preparation steps establish the accuracy and supportability of data, so there is really no need to re-establish credibility in the presentation itself.

Account Type	Average Daily Balance	Interest Earned	Average Interest Rate
Savings Account	$125.60	$0.15	0.12%
Junior	$5.32	$0.01	0.11%
Regular	$112.72	$0.14	0.13%
Holiday Savings	$7.56	$0.01	0.11%
Demand Deposit	$456.80	$1.14	0.25%
No Fee Checking	$232.75	$0.00	0.00%
Interest Bearing	$224.05	$1.17	0.52%
Certificate of Deposit	$238.20	$2.98	1.25%
6-12 month	$125.60	$1.26	1.00%
13-24 month	$75.70	$1.32	1.75%
25-36 month	$36.90	$0.83	2.25%
Total	$820.60	$4.27	0.52%

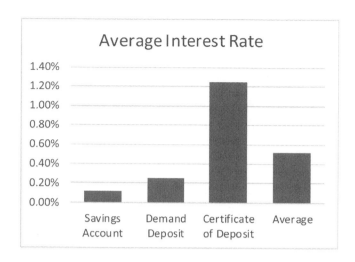

The table on the previous page shows what a typical financial institution report may look like, showing the Average Interest Rate by Account and Sub-Account Type. The Daily Balance and Interest Earned are included in the report to support the resulting Average Interest Rate metric which is based on a calculation of the previous measures. Then, members of the team can double check the calculations to verify the veracity of the Average Interest Rate metric. In a data-driven decision culture, however, metrics like Average Interest Rate have already been agreed upon, so therefore, there is only a need to display the summary data in a histogram, not verify the calculations. The chart, above, tells the same story in a simpler form. CD's earn more interest on average than all other accounts and drive the average interest rate of all accounts higher. I can quickly read the story and move on to decision-making, rather than trying to decipher all the lines in the formatted spreadsheet on the left.

The table to the left also provides more granular information than the chart on the right. Preferably, in Business Intelligence, you want to start at the most informative level of granularity, not the most detailed. In this case, the account type level provides actionable information, so there is no need to include the sub-account data in the chart. Most analytics platforms allow the user to select a higher-level aggregation, such as account type in this case, and drill-down to the next level of granularity or drill-through to the underlying raw data. The chart below shows what happens when a decision-maker drills-down on the Savings Account Column in the chart above. We now see the detailed data that is included in the spreadsheet, but we don't have to see it if it is not necessary.

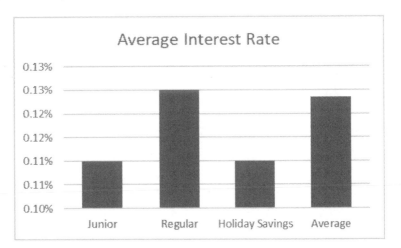

The point in choosing the right visualization for data is to make it actionable. If the data is too granular, it requires more work to arrive at a decision. If it is too detailed, information is often lost in the presentation and excluded from decision making. Properly designed visualization makes it clear what data should be considered in decision making and excludes irrelevant and/or confusing information. Having said that, it should not 'hide' data as discussed in the accuracy section of this chapter.

Visualization Technology

Once you have conquered the accuracy, accessibility and actionability of data challenges above, it is time to decide what tools will be used by your organization to support the final visualization of business intelligence. It is important to understand that your data warehouse design and underlying technology has very little to do with the visualization layer itself, beyond what has been discussed already. Visualization tools are rarely included with your investment in the data repository itself. They are separate. Another critical point to understand at this juncture is that one solution may not be enough for your organization. Your organization may find that different solutions, with different capabilities, are required to facilitate decision support throughout the enterprise. In this section, I will start at the basic and move to the more complex while explaining some of the nuances in technology that may guide your ultimate choice.

Embedded Software Reports

Many operational software products have embedded reports that provide some level of data visualization. However, there are a couple of things to consider regarding the limitations of these reports. First, operational systems usually do not have the capabilities to provide a lot of historical context. To keep these systems operating optimally, it is often necessary to eliminate access to historic data beyond a certain period. For core data processing systems, that period could be as little as six-months. The second concern with embedded reports is that they are often built as an after-thought by individuals that do not necessarily have a lot of domain expertise. Having spent some time in a software development environment myself, I am aware that the focus of many software companies are the new features that drive revenue growth. Report functionality doesn't really provide opportunities for revenue and sales growth, they are only a value-add. The people who develop software are software developers, so they don't necessarily have the experience to know what a business decision-maker needs to analyze to make a decision, unless the user specifically asks for it. In the end, the reports that you have access to in these environments are often basic or based on some other person's or entity's requirements.

Microsoft Excel and Access

Often dismissed in the universe of 'Big-Data', these products offered by Microsoft can handle a small or medium-sized financial institution's analytics needs. In fact, most of the data analytics projects that I personally do for financial institutions are completed using one, or both, these products. Again, I should note that I'm not talking about the warehousing of data here, these products would be inefficient solutions for data management on the scale required by a credit union, but for visualization they have some very useful features and, licenses for these products are already included in most Microsoft Office packages.

I have found Microsoft Access to be helpful in building small relational data bases, testing data models before deploying in SQL, and building small analytics applications, especially formatted reports. I've also used Access as an ETL processor, consuming data from various sources, translating data into a normalized format and then loading the resulting data into a SQL database. You can purchase Access add-ins from software companies than can extend Access capabilities, adding some statistics and automation capabilities that do not come with the software out of the box. FMSINC.COM, for example, has a reasonably priced add-in package that offers some productive features for Access, including the ability to automate report distribution by email and do more sophisticated statistics calculations. Admittedly, Access has limitations, has a steep learning curve for novices, and there are better solutions for a fully developed data environment, but it is a suitable place to start.

The introduction of PowerPivot and Power Query in Microsoft Excel has extended its capabilities for analyzing structured data considerably. Traditionally Excel has row and column limitations which would limit a lot of analysis on larger account portfolios. What PowerPivot and Power Query allow you to do is connect to external data and consume it in the background with virtually no limitations, except for local RAM constraints. These capabilities also allow you to use the MDX language format to build dimensions, measures and metrics on the fly that are not pre-defined in the raw dataset. So, you can add calculated columns and combine data from disparate data sources into a single analysis context. For many small and medium-sized financial institutions, these capabilities may eliminate the need for an enterprise data warehouse at the outset, keeping in mind that a data warehouse is the best solution for data storage and management. Having said that, Excel is familiar to most business

201

users and the learning curve is not quite as steep as it might be for some of the other solutions presented here.

There are also some cool analytics add-ins for Excel that extend its capabilities to rival those of much more expensive statistics products on the market. The Analysis Toolpak and Solver come with Excel but must be activated in the Add-Ins section of the software. The Analysis Toolpack allows you to do some basic statistics, such as regression analysis, and Solver allows you to run optimization scenarios. I've also used a free analytics add-in available from RealStatistics.com which provides more advanced statistical functionality. While these options may not work for more advanced or sophisticated data teams, the point is that most small and medium-sized financial institutions can do almost everything they want without spending a lot of money.

SaaS Data Analytics Platforms

When it comes to data analytics platforms that are easily connected to your data, there are plenty to choose from. I have personally used Tableau, Qlik Sense, Domo, Sisense and Power BI. They all have significant differences, but they all basically have the same features. These solutions offer the ability to connect 'live' to a variety of data sources or extract data for offline analysis, they have data visualization components onboard that you can click and drag onto a dashboard, creating pivot tables, charts, and graphs. Typically, these solutions offer an inexpensive or free desktop version, a reasonably priced cloud version for distribution of dashboards and sharing data, and a pricier server license for on-premise development which provides the organization a higher level of control and security. I should point out that these solution's strengths are not in formatted printed reports but focusing on online dashboard visualizations. Interestingly, these solutions do not require a data warehouse for implementation, can consume data from a variety of local and cloud locations and allow the user to build metrics and dimensions on the fly. This enables smaller organizations with a small data analytics budget to have, seemingly, the same power as larger organizations with more robust and sophisticated data implementations.

Tableau software has been around since 2003 and quickly became popular with companies looking to implement data-driven decision cultures using business intelligence. While it is very powerful with a lot of analytics features, my experience is that it can be complicated to use and prone to allowing critical errors that I found difficult to restore. Admittedly, this is the result of user error, but it is something to be aware of. I will also say, that I have encountered slowness in this software that I didn't experience with other offerings using the same datasets. Again, my experience was probably limited based on my level of skill. With more time and learning, I might have improved the performance, but by the time I began experimenting with this software, other less expensive, easier to use solutions had come to market. I've not revisited this software for a couple of years; things may have changed.

I haven't really used Domo or Sisense enough to provide any substantially critical review. My initial perception of Domo was that it felt a little basic. If I remember Domo's initial marketing campaign, it suggested that it would take your Excel spreadsheets to a higher level.

That was generally my perception when I tested the product. One nice thing about this offering and some of the others on this list is the ability to interact with third-party cloud data, giving your analysis some added dimension. Sisense had high-powered features and the ability to model data from disparate data sources. There was a learning curve with this one, but the output was clean and professional. At the time I tested this software, there was not an inexpensive license option like the others. The minimum cost at the time was steep for a small or medium-sized organization and they do not list any financial services clients on their website for reference.

Up until this point, I have reviewed some of the basic features of the products available for data visualization in the marketplace. As you can see, I haven't used many of these products mentioned, thus far, at any level beyond a cursory review, with the exception of Excel and Access which I think should be in any analytics team's toolbox. For that reason, I would take my comments lightly and would encourage your organization to make your own comparisons of these products. There may be features that each offer that I did not find valuable myself, but you may. My purpose is to simply make you aware that they exist. The two products below I have worked with extensively and I am a fan.

I began using QlikView, Qlik's legacy platform, in graduate school and found its statistical analysis capabilities very user friendly. I researched the product to begin using it in my own business and discovered Qlik's new cloud-based analytics platform, Qlik Sense. Qlik Sense's user-friendly features allow for quick upload or direct connection to disparate data sources, easy to define data relationships, the ability to build dimensions and metrics on the fly, and 'drag and drop' dashboard design. An individual license is inexpensive, and members of your team can build and share data and dashboards across the enterprise. Qlik also provides access to external data stores that include key economic data that can be blended with internal data for dynamic predictive analytics. I maintain a license for this platform, even though I now use Power BI for most of the dashboards that I build.

Power BI is the more recently released of these solutions, with its original retail availability coming in 2013. What was interesting about the way Power BI has been released is that it was originally released as a bare-bones platform, based on time-tested technologies incorporated in SQL Server and the features from Excel mentioned above. Over the last half decade, Microsoft has continued to release features that make Power BI a competitive Business Intelligence platform. I originally stumbled on this platform when I was searching for better charts to incorporate in Access reports. It's clear to me that Microsoft is devoting its energies to developing and enhancing Power BI to be its premier data analytics platform. The reason I migrated from Qlik to Power BI was an obvious one, simplicity. In the world of technology there are dozens of programming languages and logic that must be learned to be successful. Because Power BI is tightly integrated with the Microsoft suite of products, it represented one fewer language that I would have to learn.

Like Qlik Sense, Power BI is inexpensive for individual users, allows for direct access to data sources as well as the ability to consume data models into the cloud. There are plenty of onboard visualization components such a charts and data grids and there is a marketplace where pre-built applications for some common business projects can be obtained. One of the best features that I found beneficial is that any data model that I built in Excel can easily be integrated into Power BI. You can develop your model in a familiar platform, Excel, and then build and distribute dashboards via Power BI. In the beginning, distribution of dashboards was clunky, but that issue has been resolved and now dashboards can be shared with anyone in the universe who also has a Power BI license. If you wanted to, you could embed a Power BI dashboard into a webpage, but I will tell you that it isn't easy to do, and the results are not terrific. The one thing I find a little clunky with this software is that you don't have access to the full palette of web colors for customizing dashboards; you must create custom palettes in JSON and upload them into the software. So, you are limited to the color palette you create. Having said that, I would recommend this product to anyone starting their data journey.

****

I've mentioned five of the top eight business intelligence platforms above[40]. There are certainly many more available today and there will certainly be more to come. Business Intelligence is big business and there are a lot of players who are trying to get a piece of the market. This is good news for those undergoing transitions in their organizations today as

---

[40] https://financesonline.com/data-analytics/

the quality of available products increases and the cost of these solutions fall. Data-driven decision making is now attainable for the smallest of organizations.

As I close my argument for transformation to data-driven decision making, I want to leave you with a few important thoughts.

1. Investing in a data-driven decision culture will be transformational for your organization and provide you with a competitive edge against your slower-moving competitors.

2. Transformation must be an enterprise endeavor led from the top down.

3. Your organization will need to begin identifying team members that are data literate and begin to attract and leverage their skills.

4. The technology required for a transformation to a data-driven decision culture is readily available and relatively inexpensive.

5. Don't fall for hype!

6. Don't quit!

Appendix I

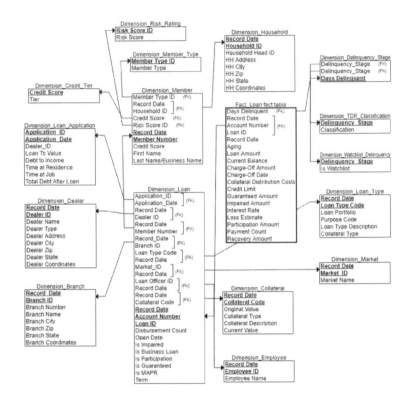

Acknowledgements

This work is derived directly from my life experience, a trajectory of events that have spanned more than a couple of decades and occurred in no particular order. In other words, I never had a plan to be an expert on credit union business intelligence. Some would argue that I still am not. My general plan, however, was to simply stay employed and pursue the things that I was interested in, but I found myself continually gravitating back to data-driven decision-making. For that reason, I think it's important to thank every business leader I have worked with or whoever tolerated my insistence on looking at the data. This list is not exclusive but includes Nancy Loftis, Scott Schmidt, Mike Kelly, Sharon Moore, Randy Smathers, Evan Etheridge, Mike James, Joe Greenwald and Tony Boutelle.

In the background, you should understand what a patient wife I have. Angie is the antithesis of a data-driven decision-maker. She lives in an entirely different world than I do. In her world, there is no risk. In my world, everything is risky. She has a tough time explaining to her friends what it is that I actually do for a living. One reason is that it constantly changes, but the critical reason is because she long ago stopped trying to understand it. One can imagine how difficult it is to live with someone who is focused 100% on a subject you have no interest in for the length of time it takes to write a book about it.˙ She is the best person I know and I'm lucky to say that she is my best friend.

Up until just a few years ago, my work with data was isolated to the silo in which I found myself, content to use data for my own benefit. Then my boss, but now a good friend, Paul Kirkbride, CLO at WESCU, unleashed my inner data geek and gave me the platform to explore some innovative ideas when it came to financial services data and providing insight to other financial institutions. Despite some strange ideas he has related to sports and music, he has become a trusted resource for advice and critical feedback.

Courtney Collier, who once worked on my data team but has become a great friend, became my data analytics muse during a critical time in my career. Courtney always gave me his honest opinion of my thoughts and ideas, provided the voice of the client that I needed to hear and embraced innovative ideas with enthusiasm. More than being a constructive force in my development, he has been a valuable cheerleader for me and has always been there to tell me to get back in the game when I was ready to quit. It was Courtney who encouraged me to write this book and if it wasn't for his encouragement I would have given up long ago.

Finally, I would like to express my sincere appreciation to all my clients and colleagues, many of which I can now call friends. I hesitate to list them, because I'm sure I would miss someone. Without their confidence in me, I would not be able to test my theories and see the results. They are the true champions of data as they have made the decision to follow the path to data-driven decision-making and given me a voice in an industry that I care passionately about.

About the Author

Michael Cochrum is the President/CEO of Creative Market Resource Group, Inc., a consultant group based in McKinney, TX that specializes in business process optimization, especially optimizing business decisions using data. Michael has almost 30 years' experience leading in highly productive organizations, including financial institutions and not-for-profits. He is a national speaker on the subject of data-driven decision making, has authored articles on the subject of data analytics and business intelligence and has written curriculum for a number of business process optimization educational courses.

Mr. Cochrum has consulted with several dozen financial institutions and software vendors over the past several years, helping his clients on their data journey. He holds a B.S. in Data Analytics from Southern New Hampshire University and an M.B.A from Texas A&M University – Corpus Christi.

Michael and his wife, Angie, reside in McKinney, TX. They are the parents of five adult children, Courtney, Andrew, Caitlin, Cassidy, and Tara. They are currently raising two German Shepherd dogs, Bella and Dixie, that they rescued in 2012 and they have two grandkids, several grand-dogs, and too many cats to count.

You can reach Michael by email at mcochrum@cmrgsolutions.com. For more information, visit www.cmrgsolutions.com.

Made in the USA
Coppell, TX
12 September 2020